Managing metadata in web-scale discovery systems

EDITED BY
Louise F. Spiteri

 facet
publishing

Published by Facet Publishing,
7 Ridgmount Street, London WC1E 7AE
www.facetpublishing.co.uk

Facet Publishing is wholly owned by CILIP:
the Chartered Institute of Library and
Information Professionals.

Every effort has been made to contact the
holders of copyright material reproduced in this
text, and thanks are due to them for permission
to reproduce the material indicated. If there are
any queries please contact the publisher.

British Library Cataloguing in Publication Data
A catalogue record for this book is available
from the British Library.

ISBN 978-1-78330-069-3 (paperback)
ISBN 978-1-78330-116-4 (hardback)
ISBN 978-1-78330-154-6 (e-book)

First published 2016

Text printed on FSC accredited material.

Typeset from editor's files by Facet Publishing
Production in 11/16 pt Palatino Linotype and
Frutiger.
Printed and made in Great Britain by CPI
Group (UK) Ltd, Croydon, CR0 4YY.

particularly in academic libraries, a number of institutional collections may not be indexed in the central library catalogue, and are thus not accessible via a central portal.

Historically, the catalogue has provided access to materials that are bought and processed within the library's system workflow. Materials that are licensed, such as e-books, pass through a different workflow and often have different processing and discovery systems associated with them. Institutionally digitized or born-digital materials have yet other workflows and systems associated with them. Institutional repositories are expanding in scope to include physical collections, digital collections, digital news feeds, course materials and syllabi, images, audio files and so forth (Balnaves, 2013). Traditional library catalogues have struggled to provide an adequate search portal to access these different resources, especially since the bibliographic records can consist of different metadata standards (more about this later).

Let us use a generic university environment to provide an illustration of a typical search environment for academic libraries. The library catalogue can provide a search portal to a number of collections that form part of the library's repository, such as:

- an e-book collection
- an e-journal collection
- a reference collection
- government documents
- audio-visual resources
- monographs
- DVDs and CDs.

The catalogue, however, may not provide access to a number of other collections made available through the library, such as:

CHAPTER 1

Introduction: the landscape of web-scale discovery

Louise F. Spiteri

Introduction: from search to discovery

An area of growing importance and concern that I address in my courses on the organization of information, as well as basic and advanced cataloguing, is the ability of our existing library metadata standards and practices to provide sufficiently robust means to manage the growing assortment of library materials available in public and especially academic libraries, including books, e-books, journal articles (print and digital), special collections, archival collections, videos, music, open access collections and so forth.

The library catalogue has typically and traditionally provided access to only parts of the collections owned by a library system, such as physical collections of books, journals, DVDs, CDs and so forth. The bibliographic records for these collections are typically structured using standard library metadata systems such as the Anglo-American Cataloguing Rules (AACR), controlled vocabularies, normally Library of Congress Subject Headings (LCSH), and encoded within the Machine-Readable Cataloging (MARC) framework. Increasingly, however,

worked as a public librarian and served as an adjunct professor at Dalhousie University, where she has taught in the areas of advanced cataloguing, reading and reading practices, and the organization of information. Her research has focused on social, interactive library catalogues and readers' advisory practices and terminology. She has released her first book, *The Library Catalog as Social Space*, and is working on her second, *Minimizing Liability and Risk in Shared Systems*. She is the recipient of the 2009 Esther J. Piercy Award from the ALA, and the 2010 Outstanding Alumni Award from the University of Alberta. laureltarulli@yahoo.com.

Aaron Tay is Library Analytics Manager at Singapore Management University. Since 2008 he has worked on various areas in the libraries such as discovery services, social media, chat services, bibliometrics and analytics. He blogs frequently at http://musingsaboutlibrarianship.blogspot.sg/, and is a big Twitter user @aarontay.

learning analytics. His current federally funded research project focuses on the development of a digital library infrastructure to address information needs in Canada's northern regions and communities. He is also investigating how learning analytics, as a big data application, supports and augments teaching and learning in learning management systems. ashiri@ualberta.ca.

Louise F. Spiteri is associate professor at the School of Information Management at Dalhousie Univeristy, Halifax, Nova Scotia. She teaches and conducts research in the areas of metadata, information management, records management, cataloguing and classification. She was a high school teacher (French and history), and worked as a cataloguer at the United Way of Greater Toronto before her move to university teaching. Her primary focus of research over the past decade has been on social catalogues, social tagging and the application of user-generated metadata to discovery systems. She serves on a variety of scholarly associations, and has served on the Board of the Association of Library and Information Science Education (2009–2011; 2015–), and is its 2016 president. She holds a BA and MA in History (York University), a Bachelor of Education (Toronto), a MLIS (Western University) and a PhD in Information Studies (Toronto). She manages the blog 'Metadata: what lies beneath' (https://simetadata.wordpress.com/), and the daily compendium *Managing Information* (https://paper.li/ f-1406205114#). For further information, please visit her page 'About Me' (https://about.me/louisespiteri). Louise.spiteri@dal.ca.

Laurel Tarulli, BMUS MLIS is the Library and Information Services Manager at Sacred Heart School of Halifax in Halifax, Nova Scotia. She is also the editor of the readers' advisory column in the ALA's professional journal *Reference & User Services Quarterly*. She has cataloguer with a strong interest in library metadata management and standards. She is a graduate of the University of Missouri Master's program in Library and Information Science. akroeger@unomaha.edu.

Heather Moulaison Sandy is assistant professor at the iSchool at the University of Missouri, where she researches and teaches in areas related to the organization of information in the digital realm, including metadata, social media use and digital preservation, and has written about these topics and presented on them nationally and internationally. Additionally, she is the co-author of two recent books (one on digital preservation, one on cataloguing with Rules for Description and Access), and editor of a column in the journal *International Information and Library Review*. She has been elected to the ALA's Council as an at-large member (2014–2017) and was elected to the nine-member conseil d'administration of the Association Internationale Francophone des Bibliothécaires et Documentalistes (2014–2017). She holds an MSLIS and an MA in Interdisciplinary French Studies, both from the University of Illinois, Urbana-Champaign, USA, and a PhD in Information Science from Rutgers University, USA. moulaisonhe@missouri.edu.

Ali Shiri is a professor at the School of Library and Information Studies at the University of Alberta, Edmonton. He completed his PhD in information science at the University of Strathclyde in Glasgow, Scotland. Previously, he worked as a senior researcher at the Centre for Digital Library Research in the University of Strathclyde. He teaches in the areas of digital libraries, and digital information organization and retrieval. His research areas centre on user interaction with digital information, digital libraries, knowledge organization systems, big data and, more recently, including Director for Innovative Technologies and Research, and as the Executive Director of the Vanderbilt Television News Archive. marshall.breeding@librarytechnology.org.

Danoosh Davoodi is an information science and technology professional with extensive research experience in the fields of linked data, library technologies, knowledge engineering and the Semantic Web. He holds a Master's degree in knowledge management, and has recently completed a Master's degree in library and information studies at the University of Alberta. He has published a book on trending semantic similarity techniques titled *Knowledge Engineering and Measure of Semantic Relatedness*. He is conducting research on modern metadata and information organization themes in the fields of digital libraries and digital preservation. danoosh.davoodi@ualberta.ca.

Christine DeZelar-Tiedman is Manager of the Archives and Special Collections Metadata Unit at the University of Minnesota Libraries, where she has worked since 2000. Prior to that she was Catalog Librarian at the University of Idaho. She received her MLIS from the University of Iowa, and is active in the Rare Books and Manuscripts Section of the Association of College & Research Libraries, and in the Association for Library Collections & Technical Services. Her many publications include articles in *Library Resources & Technical Services* and *College & Research Libraries*, as well as reviews of literary fiction in *Library Journal*, for which she was named 2016 Reviewer of the Year. Deze1002@uma.edu.

Angela Kroeger is an Archives and Special Collections Associate at the University of Nebraska at Omaha. She is a longtime

Contributors

Marshall Breeding is an independent consultant, speaker and author. He is the creator and editor of Library Technology Guides and the libraries.org online directory of libraries on the web. His monthly column 'Systems Librarian' appears in *Computers in Libraries*. He is the editor for *Smart Libraries Newsletter* published by the American Library Association (ALA), and has authored the annual *Library Systems Report* published by American Libraries since 2014. He has authored nine issues of ALA's Library Technology Reports, and has written many other articles and book chapters. He has edited or authored seven books, including *Cloud Computing for Libraries*, published in 2012 by Neal-Schuman, now part of ALA TechSource. He regularly teaches workshops and gives presentations at library conferences on a wide range of topics, and has been an invited speaker for many library conferences and workshops throughout the USA and internationally. He held a variety of positions for the Vanderbilt University Libraries in Nashville, TN, from 1985 to May 2012,

Contents

- a patent collection
- a newspaper collection (digital)
- special collections
- a thesis collection
- a map collection
- university archives.

The collections listed above do not include the bibliographic databases to which the university subscribes, and which must also be searched independently of the catalogue. Each of these collections needs to be searched separately; further, each of these collections uses its own sets of metadata standards, which may be different from those used in the library catalogue. Searching these disparate collections can be time consuming and challenging for a number of reasons. In order to conduct a comprehensive search for a particular topic, I might need to use the library catalogue, and consult the lengthy list of separate collections. This assumes that I am aware of the existence of these disparate collections, and that I have the time, patience and expertise to search them. Further, even assuming the existence of these two conditions, these disparate searches will likely require me to use external sources to manage the results I obtain from the different collections, such as a citation manager, which does not often work well with non-traditional media, e.g., audio files, or a productivity tool such as Zotero, EverNote or OneNote. Therefore I might need to juggle with several different systems and applications to keep track of, and manage, my results.

Adding further to the complexity is the variety of metadata standards and vocabularies that are used across the collections, and the lack of a common look or feel for their bibliographic records. So, for example, while a search under the controlled

Library of Congress heading **Animal welfare—Moral and ethical aspects** should result in searches with a good degree of relevance in the library catalogue, assuming, of course, that this heading has been applied correctly to the relevant titles, the Library of Congress heading for an author name, **Steiner, Gary, 1956–**, might not work as well in collections where a different name authority system is used, if one is used at all. A major underlying problem of this search environment is that the bibliographic records for these collections exist in separate indexes. This environment of disparate collections, search directories and metadata schemes places a heavy burden on the searcher, and assumes and requires a high degree of tenacity, patience, skill and, I suspect, luck.

Contrast this experience with, say, a search in Amazon, where a single search box allows me to access the myriad collections offered by this vendor via a central index, including housewares, books, films, music, software, toys and so forth. Google, of course, has become the de facto search tool used by so many people: once again, a single search box allows you to search the large and disparate variety of items indexed by Google via a central index. These web-based, centralized searches also require patience, tenacity and skill, as one might need to weed through a large number of results, but filtering options (e.g., by format in Amazon) and, one hopes, a reasonably robust relevance ranking algorithm can assist in this endeavour. At the very least, one can see the variety of sources available to search in one place; in the case of our institutional repositories, the searcher might not even know of the existence of these different collections.

The growth of web-based information resources, such as Google, Google Scholar and Amazon, and social cataloguing or reading sites such as Goodreads and LibraryThing, has served to alter significantly people's expectations of search and discovery. So, for example, if I wish to make an article-level search about a topic for scholarly research, my primary source has become Google Scholar, because of its ease of use, and the fact that I can access directly the full text of articles in journals to which my academic library has access, via a proxy server. Google Scholar is a convenient one-stop portal that includes a vast database of peer-reviewed online journals and scholarly books. Google Scholar does not allow the same level of precision as, say, databases such as Academic Search Premier, which has powerful Boolean operators, and provides the option of using controlled vocabulary. On the other hand, however, the large scope of Google Scholar could reduce my need to search different bibliographic databases to cover the same breadth of journals.

With regard to the public library catalogue, which I use for obtaining books (print and digital) and DVDs for pleasure reading and viewing, I often make my first search in Goodreads (for books), Amazon (for books and DVDs) or IMDb (the Internet Movie Database) (for DVDs), to find in-depth reviews about specific titles. Once I have decided to read or watch a particular title, I search for it in the public library catalogue. If my public library catalogue contained user reviews, or provided me with recommendations of what to read and watch, based on my history (as Goodreads and Amazon do), I would be happy to skip the step of searching an external resource and go directly to the library catalogue (see more about this in chapter 7).

Developments have been made to enable library catalogues to search across different library collections. Federated search systems were introduced in the 2000s. These systems provided one search portals to a variety of library catalogues, digital repositories and remotely hosted third-party databases. However, the potential and promise of these federated systems was not always reflected in the end results: since the bibliographic records still resided in separate indexes, searches were often slow, could produce results with high recall and low precision, and could not always cover the entire spectrum of the library's resources, such as course syllabi, newspapers and so forth (Sadeh, 2013).

Sadeh (2013) makes a good distinction between search and discovery: traditional library catalogues and databases constitute search systems, as they offered structured search interfaces tailored to the specific data they hold. Bibliographic records tend to be homogeneous, as they are constructed with the same metadata standards: these systems expect users to possess good searching literacy. Discovery systems may not offer searchers the same options to describe their information needs in detail (e.g., via the use of controlled vocabulary) but instead offer them simple search interfaces complemented with multiple post-search options for assessing findings, refining results, and navigating to other results of possible interest.

Given the 'Google effect' on searching, there have been further developments to make the library catalogue search process closer to the user experiences in web-based discovery systems such as Google, Amazon and Goodreads. Since mid-2007, a number of libraries have used what are often referred to as 'next generation catalogues', which provide a discovery layer over the central catalogue (Breeding, 2015; Han, 2012). Common examples of such discovery layers are BiblioCommons, AquaBrowser and Encore.[1] These discovery layers provide a number of features that enhance the search process, such as:

- post-search filtering of results via facets (e.g., limit by language, place, author)

- 'did you mean?' features, which can accommodate spelling mistakes and variations (e.g., grey/gray)
- the ability to save results in a personalized wish list
- relevance ranking algorithms
- one-box search
- auto-suggest for subject and author searches based on the library's authority records
- intelligent stemming
- user-generated content, e.g., tags, ratings and reviews.

While next generation catalogues are a significant improvement in the search process, the problem of decentralized indexes continues to exist, which limits their ability to search disparate collections smoothly and efficiently. The latest development, and the focus of this book, is web-scale discovery.

Web-scale discovery systems

The newest generation of the library catalogue has all the features of next generation catalogues, but with the added feature of a large central index, which brings together bibliographic records (metadata), full text, and other representations of the items in the various institutional collections. The central index is 'a component of a multi-tenant platform comprised of search and retrieval technology components, and an end-user interface. ... This group of discovery services does not exist in isolation, but as part of the ecosystem of scholarly and popular publishing, abstracting and indexing services, and in the information infrastructure of the libraries that adopt them' (Breeding, 2015, 2).

Hoy describes the core ideas of the web-scale discovery system as 'a large, vendor-supplied index of all kinds of materials coupled with a simple interface, giving patrons the ability to search across a library's entire collection quickly and easily. These services provide results in a relevance-ranked, integrated list of print, online, and multimedia content' (Hoy, 2012, 324). The primary vendors of web-scale discovery services are:

- EBSCO Discovery Service[2]
- Primo from Ex Libris[3]
- Summon from ProQuest[4]
- WorldCat Local from OCLC (the Online Computer Library Center).[5]

Web-scale discovery systems contain a number of features consistent with their web counterparts, such as relevancy-based search results, faceted navigation and user-generated content, as well as these multiple areas of functionality:

- *an end-user interface*, usually delivered via a web browser, to perform tasks such as presenting a search box for end-user queries, an alternative query page that presents advanced query options that can target terms according to structured fields, and presenting search results listed either in a brief form or in full-record displays
- *interoperability* with a link resolver to present links to full text from citation records in search results
- *local search and retrieval*, usually through an integrated indexing, search and retrieval component to collections of interest; many local search and retrieval indexes use Apache Solr (http://lucene.apache.org/solr/) or ElasticSearch (www.elasticsearch.org/) as the local search tool
- *the ability to communicate interactively* with the library's

integrated system for implementing tasks such as determining the current availability status of items in the library's physical collection, transmitting requests for holds or recalls, or interacting with the patron records to present current account status, lists of items charged, fines or fees due, or view or update personal details

- *access to remote index platforms* via an application program interface (API) in addition to, or instead of, targeting search queries and receiving results from a local index; a discovery index may also operate directly with an external platform that indexes content of interest. This interoperability is made possible through a mutually defined set of APIs that manage the requests, responses, record transfer and document presentation needed to support a search session (Breeding, 2015).

Content and structure of this book

There is no doubt that web-scale discovery systems constitute a significant and exciting development in enhancing the discovery of items in library collections. The ability to search a centralized index raises a number of questions that must be addressed, however, particularly in the management of metadata, which is the focus of this book. Depending on the library material catalogued, the discovery system needs to negotiate different metadata standards, such as AACR, Rules for Description and Access (RDA), VRA (Visual Resources Association) Core, the Metadata Encoding & Transmission Standard (METS), the Metadata Object Description Schema (MODS) and the Resource Description Framework (RDF), to name a few. How do we manage these different metadata schemes to provide a smooth and seamless discovery experience to the searchers? As web-scale discovery systems provide access to an increasing and varied amount of library resources, how do we manage metadata to help users conduct searches that result in relevant results? Do we need to be careful about the sheer volume of items to which we can provide access, so that searchers are not faced with increasingly large numbers of results at the expense of precision?

Web-scale discovery systems allow different libraries to share their metadata records widely, especially through services like WorldCat, which brings together collections from different libraries across the world. In an increasingly collaborative and cloud-based environment, what are the implications of using shared metadata? How do we maintain shared records that reflect the needs, languages and identities of culturally and ethnically varied communities? In a Google-dominated search environment, we need to provide access to library resources via a variety of non-library discovery tools. In other words, we must manage metadata within, across and outside library discovery tools by converting our library metadata to linked open data that all systems can access.

Web-scale discovery systems add further layers of metadata that are contributed by the client in the form of tags and reviews. Further, many web-scale discovery systems import user-generated metadata from external services such as Goodreads and LibraryThing. How do we manage these new types of metadata? How do we mine this metadata to better serve our members in areas such as collection development or readers' advisory?

This book examines the questions above through the lens of academic researchers and practitioners with expertise in the areas of metadata, cataloguing, bibliographic control and discovery systems. The contributing authors in the book reflect a wide array of perspectives. Christine De-Zelar Tiedman and Angela Kroeger are both practitioners in academic libraries, and manage metadata and catalogues in archives and special collections. Aaron Tay is library analytics manager at Singapore Management University, with a speciality in library discovery systems. Laurel Tarulli manages the library and information resource centre at a private school, and has previous experience managing the cataloguing department of a public library system. Danoosh Davoodi brings expertise in the areas of linked semantic data and knowledge engineering. Marshall Breeding is a very well known independent consultant, with a particular focus on library systems and technologies. Heather Moulaison Sandy, Ali Shiri and Louise F. Spiteri are researchers and faculty members in library and information science programmes, and specialize in the areas of metadata, cataloguing and linked data. More information about the authors may be found at the section on contributors at the beginning of the book.

Although all the authors, with the exception of Aaron Tay, reside and work in North America, specifically the USA and Canada, the focus of this book is not specific to any particular geographic region. By its very nature, web-scale discovery is increasingly global in scope, as resources can be linked from anywhere in the world. Throughout the book, references are made to systems that are used both within North America and beyond, and the challenges of multilingual access to global resources are addressed in more than one chapter.

Although all the chapters pertain to aspects of metadata, they can be read independently of one another; for this reason, there is a deliberate amount of overlap in content across the chapters. For example, a number of the chapters discuss the importance and impact of abstracting and indexing services, the nature of the relationship between libraries and web-scale discovery system vendors, and the National Information Standards Organization (NISO) Open Discovery Initiative report (NISO, 2014). It would, in fact, be extremely difficult to eliminate these common themes in the chapters; however, these common themes are viewed from a unique lens that reflects the focus of each chapter.

Below is a summary of themes of the chapters in the book, as well as of the major questions they address:

- *Chapter 2: Sharing metadata across discovery systems*: As we increasingly use web-scale discovery systems to help clients find a wide assortment of library materials, how do we manage the different metadata schemes used to describe these different materials? This involves the concept of mapping within and across collections, depending on the scope of the collection. How do we manage these mappings to provide seamless discovery? How do we create, maintain and share records that reflect the needs, languages and identities of culturally and ethnically varied communities?

- *Chapter 3: Managing linked open data across discovery systems*: By converting our library catalogue records to linked open data, people can discover library resources across different discovery tools, within and external to the library, which take advantage of full text search and Semantic Web technology and standards (e.g., RDF). This involves going beyond integrated discovery systems, which bring together varied resources within libraries, to what can be called 'pan discovery systems', which allow us to link our metadata records across different discovery systems. In a library context, practical linked open data applications are as of yet few in number, of limited maturity, and relatively untested. There are different semantic options available for encoding catalogue records in RDF, and to date there is little consistency in metadata schemas selected (beyond the use of RDF itself). This semantic heterogeneity complicates interoperability.

- *Chapter 4: Redefining library resources in discovery systems*:
  Given the increased scope of web-scale discovery systems, it
  is important to reconsider and redefine what we mean by
  library resources. Should the web-scale discovery systems
  link also to human resources in the library, such as expertise
  of staff, research projects conducted under the purview of the
  library, and related social media links (e.g., tags, hashtags and
  so on, related to relevant content)? Should we continue to
  rely on the library website to provide access to services, as
  distinct from the catalogue, which provides access to
  collections? If we want truly integrated discovery systems,
  should we consider making these connections seamless –
  services and collections accessed via the catalogue? What
  would this mean to managing metadata? How would we
  incorporate metadata about library services in the catalogue?
- *Chapter 5: Managing volume in discovery systems*: The well
  established measures of recall and precision are becoming
  increasingly relevant in web-scale discovery systems. Given
  the way that most people search, which is the simple
  keyword box that searches all text anywhere in the record,
  web-scale discovery systems will lead to increasingly large
  recall as we provide access to more linked items. Do we need
  to be careful about the sheer volume of items to which we can
  provide access via web-scale discovery systems? Do we want
  these systems to become another Google, where precision of
  results is not always as accurate as we would like? Are we too
  obsessed with the notion of providing access to everything at
  the expense of the quality of the results?
- *Chapter 6: Managing outsourced metadata in discovery systems*:
  The increasing reliance of vendors to provide metadata and

indexing is something we need to examine. Vendors who provide both metadata and discovery layers might not share their data with another discovery vendor; so, for example, if EBSCO produces metadata for its records but your institution does not use the EBSCO web-scale discovery system, you may not receive any metadata records. How do we negotiate metadata outsourcing for web-scale discovery systems, and how do we ensure the provision of accurate and comprehensive metadata?

- *Chapter 7: Managing user-generated metadata in discovery systems*: Web-scale discovery systems allow for the blending of metadata generated by actual library clients, and reviews or tags imported from outside sources such as Goodreads and LibraryThing. How are we mining this information? Are we simply uploading these data into our discovery systems and leaving them there purely for viewing purposes, or are we actually mining the data they contain to help us connect with our users, help build more user-centric vocabularies, create community-based reading suggestions and so forth? Our focus tends to be on managing library metadata that we create, but how are we managing user-contributed metadata, including any we import from services such as Goodreads and LibraryThing? Are we looking at trends revealed by this social data? Are we using these metadata to improve library-contributed metadata, connect with our clients, and create shared communities?

References

Balnaves, E. (2013) From OPAC to Archive: integrated discovery and digital libraries with open source. In *IFLA World Library and*

Information Congress 2013 – Singapore – Future Libraries: infinite possibilities, International Federation of Library Associations and Institutions, http://library.ifla.org/79/1/108-balnaves-en.pdf.

Breeding, M. (2015) *The Future of Library Resource Discovery: a white paper commissioned by the NISO Discovery to Delivery (D2D) Topic Committee*, National Information Standards Organization, www.niso.org/apps/group_public/download.php/14487/future_library_resource_discovery.pdf.

Han, M.-J. (2012) New Discovery Services and Library Bibliographic Control, *Library Trends*, **61** (1), 162–72.

Hoy, M. B. (2012) An Introduction to Web-Scale Discovery Systems, *Medical Reference Services Quarterly*, **31** (3), 323–9.

NISO RP-19-2014, *Open Discovery Initiative: promoting transparency in discovery*, National Information Standards Organization, www.niso.org/workrooms/odi/.

Sadeh, T. (2013) From Search to Discovery. In *IFLA World Library and Information Congress 2013 – Singapore – Future Libraries: infinite possibilities*, International Federation of Library Associations and Institutions, http://conference.ifla.org/past-wlic/2013/ifla79.htm.

Notes

1 See www.bibliocommons.com/, www.proquest.com/products-services/AquaBrowser.html, and Encore, www.iii.com/products/sierra/encore.

2 www.ebscohost.com/discovery.

3 www.exlibrisgroup.com/category/PrimoOverview.

4 www.proquest.com/products-services/The-Summon-Service.html.

5 www.oclc.org/worldcat-local.en.html.

CHAPTER 2

Sharing metadata across discovery systems

Marshall Breeding, Angela Kroeger and
Heather Moulaison Sandy

As we increasingly use web-scale discovery systems to help clients find a wide assortment of library materials, how do we manage the different metadata schemes used to describe these different materials? This involves the concept of mapping within and across collections, depending on the scope of the collection. How do we manage these mappings to provide seamless discovery? How do we create, maintain and share records that reflect the needs, languages and identities of culturally and ethnically varied communities?

The importance of sharing across library silos

Patrons are looking for easy access to curated, high quality materials through the library, yet until somewhat recently, libraries have struggled with showcasing the extent of their digital collections. Accessing the variety of digital and digitized library contents required visiting a number of electronic resources, including the online library catalogue, licensed journal articles in specialized library databases, institutional repository contents, and the contents of curated resources available on the web or through other systems. Barriers to searching these disparate systems included how content was indexed, retrieved and displayed. Before patrons could begin to search these systems, they had to know the systems even existed.

One early solution to the problem of siloed information was the use of federated searching. With federating searching, patrons could query multiple databases, and have results retrieved for each. Sophisticated federated search engines de-duplicated the results if indeed a hit was found in more than one resource. Federated searching is slow, however, and requires that a number of web-based databases respond quickly to a query. Federated searching was a marked improvement over system-by-system queries, but it was fraught with problems nonetheless.

The advent of the current generation of discovery systems that rely on large-scale central indexes generated from content representing the broad range of databases, electronic journal collections, as well as metadata describing local physical and digital collections, brings an important advancement over federated search applications that prevailed previously. These federated search platforms relied on casting search queries to multiple content targets to receive and display results to users. The search architecture of federated search lacked the speed and control of search results now possible with index-based discovery services. This newer approach dramatically changes the way that libraries make available to their clients the many different forms of content and resources that comprise their physical and electronic collections. Interoperability in discovery systems now has the potential to permit access in new and exciting ways into the future. For the work with digital libraries to reach its potential, a number of standards need to be in place, including ones governing metadata supporting search and retrieval in discovery systems. In this chapter, we begin by providing clear definitions of relevant discovery terminology. Next, we describe some of the challenges with metadata within systems, including mapping between and within the library's disparate collections. We close with a look at how metadata might better support use by varied communities, specifically with the example of access to non-English-language content.

Discovery terminology

This broad category of products focuses on the discovery or exploration of library collections via search and retrieval technologies, as well as browsing through lists or other user-interface techniques. Discovery products differ from other categories of user-oriented products.

Library catalogues

Library catalogues provide the patron in the interface of an integrated library system; such systems are defined as 'robust clusters of systems involving every process and module related to library operations' (Kinner and Rigda, 2009, 401), and include specialized interfaces for service departments dealing with print collections, such as acquisitions, cataloguing and circulation. The public-facing part of the integrated library system is the online library catalogue. The scope of a library catalogue is defined primarily by the collections managed by the integrated library system. As an integral part of the integrated library system, the online catalogue delivers functionality directly tied to its functional and organizational structure. Online catalogues generally use proprietary mechanisms for gaining access to the bibliographic description, holdings and inventory control data, and circulation status. To support online requests and other services, online catalogues have direct access to the patron profile managed within the integrated library system. Since online catalogues provide access only to the material managed by the integrated library system, they can provide features such as browsing and related references based on authority records.

Federated search products

Federated search products enable users to search multiple resources simultaneously via a search architecture that involves distributing a query to each defined target, receiving records and presenting the results. These products rely on search and retrieval protocols such as Z39.50[1] and its variants SRW/SRU,[2] or through application programming interfaces to initiate requests and receive responses between the federated search application and each resource target. Federated search products continue to be used in specialized environments, but are no longer widely used to support general search for libraries. The architecture of these products may not scale to the many hundreds of resources to which a library might subscribe, and the real-time requests and responses among these targets function more slowly than users tolerate. Federated search has been largely displaced in academic libraries by index-based discovery services. Metasearch is often used as an alternative term for federated search.

Index-based discovery services

Index-based discovery services, sometimes also called web-based discovery services, provide a broad search capability based on massive indexes derived from the universe of content of interest to libraries. The producers of index-based discovery services make arrangements with publishers to receive copies of content to be indexed. These central indexes can also be supplemented with indexes representing a library's print holdings or local digital collections. The reliance on indexes generated before a search enables these products to deliver search results rapidly, and to sort materials spanning many different sources according to relevancy. Index-based discovery services aim to provide a single search box that addresses a broad representation of library resources, and to provide an experience similar to what is available via internet search engines. The producers of these services work to index the broadest representation of the body of scholarly content available globally, which can be scoped for any given implementation to return only results that correspond to the materials available from that library. Examples of index-based discovery services include Ex Libris Primo, ProQuest Summon, EBSCO Discovery Service and OCLC WorldCat Discovery Service.[3] These products are especially oriented to academic and research libraries. Google Scholar also has many characteristics of index-based discovery services; for example, both aggregate content from disparate providers, both provide single search-box queries, and both present a 'simplified, fast, all-inclusive, and principally online research experience' (Asher, Duke and Wilson, 2013, 464).

The central index of an index-based discovery service is the component of the service that is created by ingesting and indexing the content from content providers. The indexes include the terms, phrases or keywords derived from the content provided by the publisher. These central indexes, which address an almost comprehensive portion of the body of scholarly and professional content from publishers globally, represent over one billion content items.

The manner in which central indexes are populated is a major factor to be considered for the libraries that rely on these products. The Open Discovery Initiative (ODI) was formed by the National Information Standards Organization (NISO) to explore a variety of topics related to index-based discovery with the goal to make the process more transparent. NISO published *NISO RP-19-2014, Open Discovery Initiative: promoting transparency in discovery* as a recommended practice for discovery service creators and content providers (NISO, 2014a).

Discovery interfaces

A discovery interface provides a user experience that enables patrons to search and explore library collections. Components of the discovery interface include a search box in which a patron enters a query, lists of results produced in response to a query, facets of terms or keywords to limit result sets, the presentation of a complete description of a resource, and the ability to view or link to the resource itself. A discovery interface brings together a variety of features and technologies related to search and retrieval to provide a complete environment for interacting with library collections. These products may integrate with a federated search tool or a central index, or may include internal search and retrieval components and local indexes. One of the main content sources addressed by discovery interfaces is that managed by a library's integrated library system or library services platform.

Many implementations may also address other local and remote information resources. While an online catalogue is a module of an integrated library system, discovery services are not directly tied to any specific integrated library system product. Discovery interfaces are available as open source software or as proprietary products. Open source options include Blacklight and VuFind.[4] Commercial products include SirsiDynix Enterprise, Encore from Innovative Interfaces and BiblioCore from BiblioCommons.[5]

Discovery interfaces usually offer the ability to sort results according to the relevancy of results relative to the search query entered. The search engine calculates a relevancy score for each of the result candidates based on a variety of factors. Some factors relate to how well the query matches index entries, where an exact match of all the words in the right order would receive a higher score than those containing partial matches. Scores for results may also be adjusted based on indicators of their importance, such as impact factor or citation frequency, and whether the item is a primary resource or a review or derivative article. In some cases, the calculation of relevancy can be based on the profile of the searcher, giving preference to materials related to indicated topics of interest.

Discovery products aim to connect the researcher with the content items selected from the results presented. Different linking techniques can be employed. Many rely on OpenURL link resolution to dynamically create a link to the full text of a content item based on its citation metadata, the library with which the search is affiliated, and the profile of subscriptions of that library. If the searcher is not entitled to full text access via the library's subscription profile, the link resolver may be able to offer access via other services such as document delivery, interlibrary loan, or purchasing the article from the publisher. Discovery services may also make use of smart linking or direct links, where the correct link is presented directly without the need to operate through a link resolver. In some cases, the provider of the discovery service may be able to provide access to documents via its own platform instead of linking to an external publisher via licensing agreements.

Discovery interfaces may also have the capability to provide search widgets that can be embedded in other platforms. These widgets offer specialized functionality customized to the context in which they are placed. Examples include support of a search box on a course page of a learning management system that would automatically scope the results according to the topics covered by the course.

Metadata for discovery

Metadata plays a crucial role in discovery, both in the creation of the central index, and in the operation of the discovery interface. The overall performance and accuracy in identifying search results and calculating relevancy depends on the metadata available.

Each category of content repository participating in a discovery environment is expected to provide appropriate forms of metadata. One of the challenges faced by discovery environments that address multiple types of content involves building indexes and executing search requests that function well with heterogeneous metadata. Most repositories of journal articles, for example, record authors and other contributors with initials and a last name, while metadata contained in the Machine-Readable Cataloging (MARC) framework provides full names in inverted order.

The NISO recommended practice issued by the ODI discusses in detail metadata matters that relate to discovery. The document describes the importance of metadata in discovery, advocates for transparency in metadata exchange, and makes recommendations on what metadata elements a content provider should supply to discovery service providers. The ODI stipulates a set of 15 metadata elements that content providers should supply to discovery services at a basic level (NISO, 2014a). Additional optional elements can be provided, including data from controlled vocabularies, abstracts or summaries, and the full text or transcript of the content item.

Heterogeneous representation

Discovery products usually provide access to content from multiple sources, necessitating the handling of a heterogeneous mix of metadata. The differences in the structure, quality and completeness of the metadata may diverge considerably among sources, or there may only be nuances of differences. Since it is expected that discovery tools treat content evenly and objectively in the way that results are returned and prioritized, how they manage metadata is a major factor.

Discovery products follow different strategies for metadata. ProQuest Summon, for example, maintains a single record for each unique resource. When that resource, or metadata describing it, is available from multiple sources, records are de-duplicated, and any unique elements are consolidated. EBSCO Discovery Service, in contrast, maintains separate metadata records for each representation of an item. Several categories of metadata play a role in the discovery ecosystem.

Granularity of representation

Web-scale discovery systems provide granular access to resources. In dealing with serials and periodicals, online catalogues operate at the title and holdings level. An online catalogue of an integrated library system can identify whether a library has access to a given journal title, and the years of coverage available, but cannot search for the individual articles published in those titles. Discovery services, in contrast, index individual articles, providing access points for citation elements at a minimum, with full text indexing when possible. As with monographs, online catalogues provide access for the work as a whole, while discovery services are more likely to include metadata that describes each chapter, and may also have full text for the chapters of an e-book. These distinctions are not absolute. Some online catalogues may provide metadata that describes selected articles or book chapters, and discovery services may be inconsistent in their coverage of e-book chapters.

Citation elements

Whether provided via a MARC record, through the use of a common descriptive metadata schema such as the Dublin Core Metadata Element Set,[6] or as simple data files, discovery services create their indexes based on descriptive metadata. Elements such as the title, authors and contributors, publisher name and journal title provide the fundamental access points required for discovery. These elements have few restrictions relative to intellectual property and may be provided by either primary publishers or secondary sources.

Normalization

Each of these descriptive elements may be subject to inconsistencies or inaccuracies that need to be resolved by the discovery service provider to provide reliable and consistent results. For example, names of publications can be inconsistent because of title changes, differences in abbreviation conventions, or errors. The processing workflow of discovery services includes some type of normalization to resolve inconsistencies on ingestion and indexing. Normalization can be largely automated, building rule statements based on errors or inconsistencies previously encountered. These automated processes may be supplemented by human effort and other processes related to quality control.

Identifiers

Another category of metadata involves unique identifiers. These elements play an essential role in organizing indexes for unique works, for the presentation of related materials, and for linking to, or displaying, the full text or other digital representation. For scholarly articles, the digital object identifier (DOI) uniquely identifies each work, and when available, facilitates OpenURL-based linking or direct linking for presentation or download. Critical identifiers at the journal or monograph title level include the ISSN (International Standard Serial Number) or ISBN (International Standard Book Number).

Discovery services also benefit from any mechanism that can resolve or uniquely identify authors and contributors. Personal and corporate names are handled in different ways among the different communities that describe resources, such as cataloguing departments of libraries, abstracting and indexing services, and citation management services. Multiple initiatives provide unique identifiers for authors, such as the International Standard Name Identifier (ISNI; ISO 27729:2012) and Open Researcher and Contributor ID (ORCID; http://orcid.org). Proprietary platforms such as Elsevier's Scopus (www.scopus.com/) employ unique author identifiers. The Virtual International Authority File (VIAF; https://viaf.org/) is an example of a service that combines references to a unique name from multiple authoritative sources.

Abstract and indexing

Abstracting and indexing services participate in the discovery ecosystem in a more complex way. These services are usually created as proprietary products, produced through the efforts of skilled personnel. Specialists review descriptive metadata, assign terms from controlled vocabularies, and may write summaries or abstracts. The records created through this process are aggregated into specialized databases or resources, which are then made available through commercial subscriptions. While abstracting and indexing products include some of the most valuable metadata, their producers are often reluctant to contribute to web-scale discovery services; such inclusion could lead to a devaluation of their abstracting and indexing products. The production of these services depends on the income generated through subscriptions, and there is concern that libraries may not maintain their subscriptions if that content is freely available in a discovery service. In order to contribute to a discovery service, abstracting and indexing providers usually require that their content not be made available freely, but must be restricted to authenticated users from subscribing institutions. When available, content from abstracting and indexing products can significantly improve discovery through the controlled vocabulary terms and abstracts that are often produced with the expertise of subject specialists.

The full text of a work can also be indexed by a discovery service, allowing every word and phrase to function as an access point. Full text indexing is a feature of most specialized academic resources, and users are acclimated to expect to search on any word in a text via internet search engines. Inclusion of full text in a web-scale discovery service provides useful functionality, but often with undesirable side-effects. The number of false or weak hits returned increases. An article with indexed full text of more distant relation to the query terms may appear higher in a result set than one more on target represented only by citation metadata. The discovery services that include full text have to address these issues in the algorithms used to calculate relevancy.

Use metrics can also inform relevancy calculations and help users identify important works. These metrics might include the number of times that the resource has been cited. Statistics on the number of times a resource is accessed on the discovery platform may also provide data to identify or sort items of relative importance. These metrics naturally change constantly, and must be interrogated dynamically or at least updated frequently.

Use data can also identify relations among resources that may not be apparent through descriptive metadata. The bX Recommender Service from Ex Libris,[7] for example, mines the logs of link resolution servers to capture use patterns. Articles selected during a discrete search session by a researcher have some probability of being related. This inferential metadata may not be specific enough to impact the identification of result candidates and relevancy, but can be helpful to drive optional functionality, such as a service to display related items.

Mapping materials from within and across collections

Metadata mapping is one solution to the problem of integrating disparate material from wildly divergent sources, such as MARC-based library catalogues, databases using a variety of metadata standards such as Metadata Object Description Schema (MODS) and XML (Extensible Markup Language), library web pages in HTML (Hyper Text Markup Language), course management software in proprietary formats, e-books in EPUB, PDF and other formats, and other types of information resources encoded to be retrievable in their native environments. For the purposes of this chapter, we are speaking of descriptive metadata, which describes the content of the resource (typically including information such as title, author, date, topic, and more), and the metadata encoding schema, which wraps this descriptive metadata into a machine-readable form.

Each domain or publishing sector that produces content relies on different metadata formats or standards, each with distinct metadata syntax, descriptive elements and vocabularies. Each metadata standard was designed to fulfil a specific set of needs, usually without consideration of compatibility with other metadata standards used by other disciplines or industries. In a discovery environment, libraries attempt to bring all of these diverse types of metadata together and make it accessible via a single search box. The quest to improve interoperability between such disparate systems may be likened to herding cats.

Mapping and crosswalks

Metadata maps and crosswalks are the most common methods used to achieve interoperability. While some people use the terms 'mapping' and 'crosswalking' nearly interchangeably, they are distinct concepts, albeit closely related. The J. Paul Getty Trust defines 'metadata mapping' as 'a formal identification of equivalent or nearly equivalent metadata elements or groups of metadata elements within different metadata schemas, carried out in order to facilitate semantic interoperability' (2008, 3), and a 'crosswalk' as:

> a chart or table (visual or virtual) that represents the semantic mapping of fields or data elements in one data standard to fields or data elements in another standard that has a similar function or meaning. Crosswalks make it possible to convert data between databases that use different metadata schemes and enable heterogeneous databases to be searched simultaneously with a single query as if they were a single database (semantic interoperability). Also known as field mapping.
>
> J. Paul Getty Trust, 2008, 1

In other words, mapping is the 'intellectual activity' of determining the semantic equivalency between elements in different metadata schemas, while crosswalks are the tangible output of that activity (Woodley, 2008).

The principal uses for crosswalks are 'to convert data to a new or different standard, to harvest and repackage data from multiple resources, to search across heterogeneous resources, or to merge diverse information resources' (Woodley, 2008, 2–3). For any scenario in which metadata from different sources is brought together into a common system, the key to interoperability is accurately mapping the data from the source to the target (Godby, Young and Childress, 2004; Zeng and Chan, 2006).

Direct mapping of equivalent or similar terms (elements,

fields or tags) is the main method of building a crosswalk (Chan, 2005). A simple, straightforward, one-to-one correspondence between all terms of two different metadata schemas is extremely rare, if not unheard of. Typically, any two metadata schemas have inherently different levels of granularity, and multiple fields from the more detailed and complex schema may be mapped to a single field of the less complex schema (Chan, 2005; Woodley, 2008). Therefore when complex schemas are converted to simpler ones, granularity and actual data values are lost (Zeng and Chan, 2006).

A wide variety of complications, near matches, and non-matches can occur with any crosswalk, including the following scenarios:

- Elements in either the source or target schema are modified by qualifiers and sub-elements (Zeng and Chan, 2006). For example, a topical element in the source schema may have a geographic or date qualifier, which is lost in a target schema that has no provisions for qualifiers.
- Elements in the source and target schemas 'overlap in meaning and scope' (Zeng and Chan, 2006, section 4.3).
- A non-repeatable source element maps to a repeatable target element, where the source element may contain multiple values separated by a designated character (semicolons are common), which need to be mapped to multiple iterations of the target element (St Pierre and LaPlant, 1998).
- A repeatable source element maps to a non-repeatable target element, which results in loss of data or in designing the crosswalk to place multiple values into the same target element.
- A single source element maps to multiple unique target

elements (St Pierre and LaPlant, 1998).

- Multiple source elements map to a single target element (St Pierre and LaPlant, 1998).
- A source element has no matching or nearly matching target element to which it may be mapped, resulting in either loss of data, or mapping to a target element defined for some other type of content (St Pierre and LaPlant, 1998; Woodley, 2008).
- The source schema has no corresponding element to fill a mandatory element of the target schema (St Pierre and LaPlant, 1998).
- The source database may contain 'hybrid records' that describe both an original resource and its replica or surrogate on the same record (Woodley, 2008). For example, a book and a PDF scanned from the book, an artefact, a digital photograph of that artefact, a reel-to-reel audio tape, and a CD reproduction of the recording, etc., described on the same resource record, even though these constitute different formats with different means of discovery and retrieval.
- Records in the source database may be composites constructed according to different and conflicting content standards (Woodley, 2008). This could be a catalogue with a mix of records catalogued with different content standards, such as the Anglo-American Cataloguing Rules (AACR2) and Resource Description and Access (RDA). In a more extreme, but not uncommon, situation this could be a catalogue or database that has already had marginally compatible records crosswalked into it in the past, which must be crosswalked again into yet another schema. Crosswalks are human- or computer-readable documents

that map metadata elements between
different metadata standards (Marine Metadata
Interoperability, n.d.). For example, records that started as
Encoded Archival Description (EAD) and were crosswalked
into MARC and are now moving to Dublin Core. If any of
the elements had suboptimal mapping in the EAD-to-MARC
transition, the second transition will likely further increase
the gap between the element definition and the data
contained within it.

- The two element sets may have different hierarchical
  structures, or one of them may have a flat, non-hierarchical
  structure (Woodley, 2008).

Element-to-element mapping is only one part of a well developed
crosswalk. In addition, content standards and controlled
vocabularies must be considered (Woodley, 2008). For example,
if the two schemas use different controlled vocabularies for
names, a name that is correctly formatted for the source schema
may be incorrectly formatted for the target schema. For example,
the name of the author of *The Tale of Genji* is formatted as
'Murasaki Shikibu, 978?-' by the US Library of Congress, but as
'Murasaki Shikibu 0978?-1016?' by the Bibliothèque nationale de
France. To a human reader, these are obviously the same name,
but to a computer, the different formatting of the date results in
a mismatch. So, in addition to mapping the data structure from
one schema to another, it may be necessary to map the data values
as well (Woodley, 2008). In order to match a query using one
controlled vocabulary to results using a different controlled
vocabulary, a discovery system must implement some form of
internal cross-concordance (Kempf et al., 2014).

Content providers working with libraries need to be aware that their metadata may be crosswalked into a discovery system, and that their resources may not be searchable to the same level of detail in the discovery system as they would be in their database's native search interface. Likewise, discovery service providers should attempt to be transparent about their metadata mapping and crosswalks, so that librarians and content providers can better understand how the imported content is searched and presented by the discovery service. The conformance checklists published by the ODI for both groups are an attempt to clarify how metadata is encoded and how it can be used by the discovery service.

Methods for transferring metadata

Two common methods for transferring metadata into discovery systems are File Transfer Protocol (FTP) and the Open Archives Initiative Protocol for Metadata Harvesting (OAI-PMH) (Hoeppner, 2012). FTP is a simple, widely used protocol for moving any kind of data or metadata from one computer or network to another. OAI-PMH is explicitly tailored to the transfer of descriptive metadata using the Dublin Core Metadata Element Set, and is used to gather together metadata descriptions from multiple repositories into a central index. For discovery systems that use a central index, the library may be required to supply all of the MARC-encoded records from their catalogue, which may be mapped into the metadata format preferred by the vendor; this format may or may not be proprietary (Hoeppner, 2012). The records that have been crosswalked from MARC may then be loaded into the central index via FTP. Meanwhile, OAI-PMH may be employed to harvest metadata from other library resources, which includes digitized materials, from institutional repositories (Hoeppner, 2012). OAI-PMH has been recently superseded by

ResourceSync, a synchronization framework developed by NISO and OAI.[8] Whether via FTP, OAI-PMH, ResourceSync or some other mechanism, the metadata from these different sources are brought together in the central index.

For discovery systems using knowledge bases and OpenURL link resolvers (described earlier), the recommended practice from the Knowledge Bases and Related Tools (KBART) Phase II Working Group is for content providers to supply data in the KBART data format, which is a simple tab-delimited UTF-8 text file (NISO, 2014b). This requires content providers to map whichever metadata format they normally use to the KBART field (NISO, 2014b). It is easy to map metadata from a complex schema – whichever schema the content provider may be using – to a simple schema, as long as there is no need to later map the same metadata back into a complex schema (either the original schema or some other complex schema). The KBART fields are designed to be simple, and to capture the most common metadata elements that can be reasonably expected to exist in some form or another across many standards. KBART fields include such things as *publication_title, print_identifier* (e.g., ISSN or ISBN), *first_author, publisher_name* and others (NISO, 2014b). The KBART data format includes 25 fields, including some that apply only to serials or only to monographs, so that not every field would be needed for every resource. The simplicity of the KBART data format allows it to serve as a type of metadata lingua franca if it achieves widespread adoption. Such standardization streamlines the process of loading new resources into discovery systems.

Metadata considerations that could hamper seamless discovery

A number of matters must be considered for integrating content described at different levels into the central index. For example, journal aggregator databases describe their constituent resources at the article level, often including full text searching. By contrast, traditional library catalogues describe resources with surrogate records, with books and journals described at the title level, minimal or no chapter or article-level description, and no full text resources (Han, 2012). In a discovery environment, where full text, article-level resources intermingle with title-level surrogate records, it can be a challenge for discovery service providers to balance their relevancy ranking algorithms to ensure that resources described with information-poor surrogate records are not completely lost in the sea of information-rich full text resources. However, resources described with surrogate records still enjoy an apparent advantage over resources not indexed at all within the discovery system. Even minimal surrogate records provide some opportunities for resources to be found, while any resources that are wholly omitted from the discovery index can never be found by those users who treat the discovery search as a one-stop-shop for research queries.

Problems and limitations

Inaccurate mapping muddles resource discovery, but mapping errors reveal patterns that may be used to trace problems. Sometimes, errors are relatively obvious, such as when an author element is mapped to a description element, and sometimes errors stem from conflating elements that seem related but which serve different roles, such as mapping 'taxon' from IEEE (Institute of Electrical and Electronics Engineers) Learning Object Metadata to 'subject' in Dublin Core (Zeng and Qin, 2008).

Not all metadata standards mandate a one-to-one relationship between the metadata record and the manifestation it describes. Even in those that do, many institutions bend the rules and use the same metadata record for a physical work and its digital copy (Woodley, 2008). Suppliers of e-resources may use print identifiers in their records (Kemperman et al., 2014). Of course, even if all elements are mapped as fastidiously as possible, there remains the problem of incomplete or incorrect values populating the metadata elements.

In 2009, the University of Nevada's Las Vegas Libraries Discovery Task Force conducted detailed staff and vendor surveys regarding discovery service needs and capabilities (Vaughan, 2012). The survey questions and staff responses were published, but vendor responses and other specific details were not made public, because of the swift rate of development in the discovery marketplace, thus rendering the information obsolete quickly. Even without the vendor responses, however, the specific questions asked of vendors provide a good overview of metadata concerns in discovery systems. The long, detailed vendor investigation survey covered topics such as:

- the size and scope of the central index
- mechanisms for including local content such as the library's catalogue, locally digitized resources, and institutional repository
- scheduling options for harvesting local metadata
- adjustability of relevancy ranking algorithms, particularly with regard to discoverability of local content
- inclusion or exclusion of specific metadata elements
- the existence of agreements with other content providers

- de-duplication of identical content supplied by multiple providers
- the ability to include open access content
- authentication, licensing and rights management
- usability.

Vaughan, 2012

One of the questions asked in the vendor survey, 'With what metadata schemas does your discovery platform work? (e.g., MARC, Dublin Core, EAD, etc.)' (Vaughan, 2012, 44), reveals the expectation that discovery systems can accommodate a variety of schemas, and acknowledges the reality that no discovery system can accommodate all schemas.

Discovery services support the ingestion of metadata created in multiple schemas, but almost always normalize it into their own internal schema. Even if a discovery system could support multiple metadata schemas without transforming them to other schemas, mapping would still be necessary to search across fields that have different labels and specifications in the different supported schemas. The more metadata that a discovery system can search in its native format, the better represented those resources will be in the search results. Often, when metadata is transformed to a common schema, a relatively simple schema may be chosen as the lowest common denominator. Thus, the central index may contain stripped-down metadata, when compared with the sources (Hoeppner, 2012).

Exclusions and gaps in coverage

Even with extensive efforts to map and crosswalk metadata, no existing discovery system on the market covers all of a library's available resources. A hybrid approach, using both a central index and federated search, can alleviate this somewhat, by using federated search to include resources that cannot be imported into the central index (Chickering and Yang, 2014). Some entire categories of resources, however, are still broadly excluded from the discovery environment.

Discovery services typically index material in library catalogues, subscription databases, and open access resources, but other information may need to be integrated, including all information on the library's website, content management systems, course management software and so forth (Breeding, 2014). Business competition may also play a role, as some companies are both database vendors and discovery service providers, and they may not include their competitors' databases in their central indexes (Hoeppner, 2012). Additionally, a number of data suppliers are reluctant or unable to contribute their metadata because of intellectual property considerations or concerns that their products will not be presented in an ideal manner (Somerville and Conrad, 2014).

Another notable weakness is the exclusion of abstracting and indexing services, which resist providing their content to discovery services (Breeding, 2015). The precise vocabularies of abstracting and indexing services often do not translate well to the discovery environment, and the providers are reluctant to put their resources into what they perceive as a suboptimal environment (Kabashi, Peterson and Prather, 2014). Open access content is another weak area, where publishers often provide insufficient metadata for open access resources, and indexers omit open access publications from coverage (Somerville and Conrad, 2014). The situation for inclusion of open access resources within discovery systems has been improving recently, however (Breeding, 2015).

Other types of resources often excluded from the discovery environment include unpublished materials, conference proceedings, archival resources, special collections, multimedia, non-textual media content such as images and videos, research data sets, special collections, analytics, altmetrics, genealogical resources, career resources, tests, tutorials, and other library resources not traditionally described with bibliographic metadata (Breeding, 2015; Kabashi, Peterson and Prather, 2014; Somerville and Conrad, 2014). It may even be argued that a truly comprehensive discovery environment would include 'full library destinations and services, including library facilities, resources, and expertise' (Somerville and Conrad, 2014). Some of these types of resources do not presently have metadata standards associated with them, and so they are beyond the scope of mapping, as there is no source schema from which to map.

Future shifts?

Dahl predicts a 'shift from library management of isolated databases to … [management of the] library's imprint on shared global discovery platforms' (2009, 8). This will come with a rise in interest in curation of resources that are unique to a given library and of global interest (Dahl, 2009). This projected shift in focus from local to global is highly relevant to discovery systems, which increasingly draw together metadata from widely varied sources. If current trends continue, local discovery systems that sit on top of integrated library systems may eventually be completely or largely supplanted by cloud-based global systems. In a global environment, the greatest challenge is bringing the library's local, unique content to the top and making it findable by niche users, while continuing to create, maintain and share records that reflect the needs, languages and identities of culturally and ethnically varied communities.

In a similar vein, Seeman and Goddard (2014) posit that creating better structured data with current library cataloguing tools will facilitate a smoother transition into the predicted linked data cataloguing environment of the future. It is important to focus the greater portion of our effort on improving shared metadata, rather than on making local enhancements that benefit only a single catalogue. Presently, most libraries import MARC records from union catalogues, national libraries, vendors and other sources into a local catalogue, when it might be more beneficial to instead link to decentralized, distributed records, which may not even be 'records' as understood today, but collections of metadata statements from multiple data stores (Seeman and Goddard, 2014). Libraries likewise recognize a need to shift focus towards unique, local resources not duplicated in the collections of other libraries (Seeman and Goddard, 2014).

The move away from local catalogues to a decentralized model will influence the functionality of discovery systems. Many discovery systems overlay an OPAC (online public access catalogue), but if there is no OPAC, the discovery systems must accommodate linked open data from the web, in addition to more traditional metadata from vendors' walled gardens. Time will tell whether this adds layers of complexity to discovery systems, or if it liberates them from having to deal with catalogue data in an obscure format (namely, MARC). This also raises the question of libraries' current efforts to move towards shared metadata on a global scale, while vendors very likely retain a strong interest in keeping close control over their metadata to protect their business interests. This conflict is already in play and is likely to become more prominent in the near future.

The global nature of discovery systems: challenges of language and support

For what purpose do we provide discovery services if not to provide access to users? Yet library users are as diverse as the information they search. The global nature of discovery systems raises a number of questions about usability, appropriateness and adequacy for users that relate directly to both the content included in the central index, and the discovery interface as presented. One overarching concern with global endeavours involving discovery is the challenge of language support.

At least four interrelated challenges can be identified on the topic of language support when considering global discovery systems. First is the question of content. Can libraries add metadata for content in the language of their users to the discovery system's central index? The question of metadata logically ties in to the question of retrieval, as content is worth nothing if it cannot be retrieved and used.

The second language-related concern has to do with the robustness of metadata that describes non-English-language content. Theoretically, if the metadata is created and adheres to standards accepted by the discovery systems, there should be no problem for end-user searching. It is unclear, however, if locally developed content outside the English-speaking world and beyond the Global North would necessarily adhere to standards for description or for encoding schema. Although a repository's metadata may be accurate and internally consistent, it might not necessarily be shareable and interoperable according to different discovery system standards and practices.

In some ways, the ODI from NISO of the USA addresses the second concern through the publication of conformance checklists for content providers mentioned previously in this chapter. Foreign-language content providers can communicate the extent to which their content can be indexed and retrieved by the discovery system through the use of the conformance checklists. These providers would download the conformance checklist template (http://bit.ly/1maaxYy), and post their responses to their websites. NISO is the national standards body for information and the book trade in the USA. Because NISO and the ODI are both US-based, only an English-language version of the checklist is available that focuses on the USA's discovery system environment.

A third concern relates to retrieval and display. Assuming content can be indexed, is it possible for users to retrieve it according to their needs? Are users able to search contents in specific languages, especially if a keyword input into the search box is spelled identically in a number of languages? In some cases, novice researchers may prefer content in their native language, but advanced researchers might be more knowledgeable of English-language treatment of their subject area, and prefer to see international (e.g., non-English-language) results. If users cannot limit their results to a specific language within the discovery system, the results set has the potential to promote frustration in lieu of discovery.

Finally, challenges with language support in discovery systems include educating librarians on the back-end expertise required to make front-end discovery happen. Librarians need to make content available through these systems, and they need to understand the systems well enough to instruct end-users. If documentation, training and user group support are not available to assist librarians in working with these materials and with their patrons, it will be more difficult to gain librarian support, as discovery systems will be perceived to be arbitrary and unpredictable (see Buck and Steffy, 2013).

Discovery system providers: efforts and initiatives

Discovery system providers are not insensitive to the global market and to the need for language support in their products. The ODI's work with conformance checklists for content providers was mentioned above. The ODI has also created conformance checklist templates for discovery service providers. Like the content providers, discovery service providers are encouraged to download the conformance checklist template, fill it out, and post it to their website.

Three discovery service providers have filled out and posted conformance checklists: Ex Libris, ProQuest and EBSCO; the fourth provider of web-scale discovery services, OCLC (the Online Computer Library Center), has not posted its conformance statement as of the writing of this chapter. One of the conformance checklist elements pertains to the library's ability to configure result sets for its users. All three major discovery service providers permit the library to 'establish preferences', to list platforms and to prioritize, at least partially. See Table 2.1.

For the purpose of this chapter, the three discovery service providers that have completed the ODI conformance checklist (Ex Libris, ProQuest and EBSCO) are considered for their ability to provide support in different languages and scripts, and for different content. Below, we look briefly at each in turn.

Ex Libris, an Israeli company that signed an agreement in October 2015 to be acquired by ProQuest, has a discovery service

Table 2.1 Conformance checklist content for three content providers

Checklist element	Ex Libris[1]	ProQuest[2]	EBSCO[3]
Mechanisms are offered to enable libraries to establish preferences regarding which platforms to present to users as link targets, and in what order or priority	Yes	Partially Preferences can be set by the library, however our system takes into consideration the 'best available link', without favouring any particular content provider, to avoid serving up broken links	Yes

[1] See www.exlibrisgroup.com/default.asp?catid={8B84715C-234A-44A9-B3C1-DCDD2E18D049}.
[2] See http://media2.proquest.com/documents/NISO+ODI+conformance+checklist+-+Discovery+Service+Provider2.pdf.
[3] See https://www.ebscohost.com/odi-conformance-checklists.

called Primo. A publicity document from 2015 (Ex Libris, 2015) states that libraries in non-English-speaking countries using Primo include ETH Zurich (www.library.ethz.ch/en), Aalborg University, Denmark (www.en.aub.aau.dk), and the Royal Library, Denmark (http://rex.kb.dk). These three libraries have sites in their native languages, along with English interfaces. A search for words in the native language that might appear only in the title or other descriptive metadata produces results that are uniformly in the native language. In a search for terms that might appear in the publisher statement, however, non-target language publications such as English-language publications can be returned as readily as native language results. A search for 'KONGELIGE' in the search box of the Aalborg University, no matter the interface used or the language selected, yielded results in English as well as in Dutch. On the first page of ten hits for 'KONGELIGE', five of these are in English.

ProQuest, a US-based company, has a discovery service called Summon. Unlike Ex Libris, ProQuest is a discovery service provider as well as a content provider. As early as 2013, ProQuest reported working with international, non-English publishers Minha Biblioteca, Universitetsforlaget AS and Boom uitgevers Den Haag, with the intention of including their content in Summon's central index (PR Newswire, 2013). According to the ProQuest blog (2015), the Universidad de Murcia library[9] has opted to use Summon as its discovery service. In an informal search of the discovery service, a Spanish-language word, 'Internacional', was searched; however, only nine of the first ten results were in Spanish. Consistent searching in a particular language, therefore, is not assured in Summon, either.

EBSCO, another US-based company, has a discovery service called EBSCO Discovery Services (EDS). EBSCO, like ProQuest, is also a content provider, offering a number of article databases to subscribers. EDS supports language translation for certain EBSCO-sourced HTML articles. On its Success Stories (EBSCO, 2015) web pages, EBSCO publishes stories about libraries using different products the company offers. A university in South Korea reports increasing the use of library e-resources after implementing EDS (EBSCO Information Services, 2016a). It mentions the importance of having access to Korean e-resources, and the library's implementation is in Korean[10] and English. The University of St Gallen (HSG) in Switzerland also uses EDS (EBSCO Information Services, 2016b). As with Summon, after the system[11] is searched, results are displayed on a page where users can modify the language of the interface. But also as with Summon and Primo, a search for the German-language term 'Instrumente' yields two English-language resources in the first ten hits.

Addressing the effects of language

The question of how to create, maintain and share records that reflect the needs, languages and identities of culturally and ethnically varied communities remains unanswered. Until recently, discovery systems have indexed curated content held in databases constructed by, or licensed through, libraries. Some of these databases are proprietary, and content is paid. Other resources, such as the HathiTrust (www.hathitrust.org), make some content available openly, but charge for other content. The push towards interoperability and openness has paved the way for multi-institutional initiatives to emerge. In the USA, structured initiatives such as the Digital Public Library of America (DPLA) provide assistance to institutional members through the creation of hubs that allow open content from individual institutions to be freely searched through the DPLA interface (http://dp.la). Europeana, the European predecessor to DPLA, also provides federated search for a number of institutions' content, but in Europeana that content is provided by nearly 150 content providers working in a number of non-English languages.[12] As with the discovery systems investigated, however, limiting the language of results in Europeana exists only as a post-search facet. Additionally, resources such as the repositories listed in the Directory of Open Access Repositories (OpenDOAR, 2015) make their contents open to federated search,[13] and potentially to harvesting. Worldwide, 2961 repositories (OpenDOAR, 2015) have opened their contents to the OpenDOAR search, meeting basic requirements for interoperability and sharability (Shreeves, Riley and Milewicz, 2006).

In the future, discovery service providers will need to continue to meet the needs of a diverse user base of international partner libraries; in doing so, finding and sharing international content will increasingly become a priority. Although an argument could be made that much of the world's research is published in English-language venues, researchers in non-English-speaking areas should have the right to select the language of the results of their search as part of their basic query. The needs of diverse researchers can be addressed to some extent through the customization of the discovery service interface, but if the content of the central index does not meet their needs, the exercise of providing a usable discovery interface lacks purpose.

Sharing metadata across different integrated discovery systems could potentially be seen as a method for mitigating the problem of a dearth of non-English-language content. It will be up to the discovery service providers, however, to streamline the addition of local content, to support non-English-language searching more thoroughly, and to connect libraries with curated, open content in ways libraries and their users have never before imagined.

Conclusion

Libraries have been sharing metadata since before the internet existed, sharing printed catalogue cards via subscription service, and publishing bound volumes of their catalogues, with records that could be manually copied onto catalogue cards. The internet has transformed metadata sharing from a helpful convenience into an absolute necessity. The sheer volume of library resources, especially vast databases of electronic resources purchased or leased by libraries, makes manual input of metadata by individual libraries impossible. One library or vendor creates the metadata, and then others copy or import that metadata into their catalogues, integrated library systems or discovery systems.

Metadata for entire collections must be migrated in bulk, typically without the luxury of checking the quality of more than a small sampling of the records.

The need to share metadata across diverse systems is a pervasive fact of everyday library operations. Because metadata is created according to a variety of different descriptive standards, however, the use of a variety of different metadata schemas among systems, and created by different vendors, causes problems with metadata compatibility or interoperability. Libraries, of course, want their users to have a seamless experience, and the ability to search all of a library's available resources and retrieve all of the resources best suited to their needs. The unfortunate reality is that no discovery system available can truly ingest all types of metadata smoothly, nor search them with equal efficacy, nor present them to users without both missing some relevant items, and including some irrelevant items. Additionally, the needs of non-English-language searchers need to be better accommodated through the use of interoperable metadata and responsive discovery interfaces.

Libraries, content providers and discovery service providers, all have an interest in improving the current situation. One way to improve interoperability effectively is for all involved parties to agree to adhere to common standards. Standards allow us to move beyond what individual libraries, projects and collections are doing to participate in international projects and initiatives, and to place all sources on an equal footing.

References

Asher, A. D., Duke, L. M. and Wilson, S. (2013) Paths of Discovery: comparing the search effectiveness of EBSCO Discovery Service,

Summon, Google Scholar, and conventional library resources, *College & Research Libraries*, **74** (5), 464–88.

Breeding, M. (2014) Library Resource Discovery Products: context, library perspectives, and vendor positions, *Library Technology Reports*, **50** (1), 5–58.

Breeding, M. (2015) *The Future of Library Resource Discovery: a white paper commissioned by the NISO Discovery to Delivery (D2D) Topic Committee*, National Information Standards Organization, www.niso.org/apps/group_public/download.php/14487/ future_library_resource_discovery.pdf.

Buck, S. and Steffy, C. (2013) Promising Practices in Instruction of Discovery Tools, *Communications in Information Literacy*, **7** (1), 66–80.

Chan, L. M. (2005) Metadata Interoperability: a study of methodology, *Chinese Librarianship: An International Electronic Journal (CLIEJ)*, **19**, www.iclc.us/cliej/cl19.htm.

Chickering, F. W. and Yang, S. Q. (2014) Evaluation and Comparison of Discovery Tools: an update, *Information Technology & Libraries*, **33** (2), 5–30.

Dahl, M. (2009) The Evolution of Library Discovery Systems in the Web Environment, *OLA Quarterly*, **15** (1), www.scribd.com/doc/14690604/Evolution-of-Library-Discovery-Systems-in-the-Web-Environment#scribd.

EBSCO (2015) *Success Stories*, www.ebsco.com/success-stories.

EBSCO Information Services (2016a) EBSCO Discovery Service API helps University in South Korea Increase Use of Library E-resources: Namseoul University, http://bit.ly/1mabMH4.

EBSCO Information Services (2016b) EBSCO Discovery Service Increases Searches and Full-text Downloads at Swiss University: University of St. Gallen (HSG), Switzerland, http://bit.ly/1mabWOF.

Ex Libris (2015) *Discovery beyond Searching: innovative ways of using Primo: examples from 10 institutions around the globe*, www.exlibrisgroup.com/files/AboutUs/InnovativeWaysofUsing PrimoBrochure.pdf.

Godby, C. J., Young, J. A. and Childress, E. (2004) A Repository of Metadata Crosswalks, *D-Lib Magazine*, **10** (12), www.dlib.org/dlib/december04/godby/12godby.html.

Han, M.-J. (2012) New Discovery Services and Library Bibliographic Control, *Library Trends*, **61** (1), 162–72.

Hoeppner, A. (2012) The Ins and Outs of Evaluating Web-Scale Discovery Services: librarians around the world are trying to learn what WSD services are and how they work, *Computers in Libraries*, **32** (3), 6–10, 38–40.

ISO 27729:2012 *International Standard Name Identifier*, International Standards Organization.

J. Paul Getty Trust (2008) Glossary. In Baca, M. (ed.), *Introduction to Metadata, Online Edition, Version 3.0*, www.getty.edu/research/ publications/electronic_publications/intrometadata.

Kabashi, A., Peterson, C. and Prather, T. (2014) *Discovery Services: a white paper for the Texas State Library and Archives Commission*, Texas State Library & Archives Commission, www.tsl.texas.gov/sites/default/files/public/tslac/lot/TSLAC_WP_ discovery__final_TSLAC_20140912.pdf.

Kemperman, S. S., Brembeck, B., Brown, E. W., de Lange-van Oosten, A., Fons, T., Giffi, C., Levin, N., Morrison, A., Ruschoff, C., Silvis, G. A. and White, J. (2014) *Success Strategies for Electronic Content Discovery and Access: a cross-industry white paper*, Online Computer Library Center, www.oclc.org/go/en/econtent-access.html.

Kempf, A. O., Ritze, D., Eckert, K. and Zapilko, B. (2014) New Ways of Mapping Knowledge Organization Systems: using a semi-automatic matching procedure for building up vocabulary crosswalks, *Knowledge Organization*, **41** (1), 66–75.

Kinner, L. and Rigda, C. (2009) The Integrated Library System: from daring to dinosaur?, *Journal of Library Administration*, **49**, 401–17.

Marine Metadata Interoperability (n.d.) *Moving Between Standards (Crosswalking)*, https://marinemetadata.org/guides/mdatastandards/crosswalks.

NISO (2014a) *NISO RP-19-2014 Open Discovery Initiative: promoting transparency in discovery*, National Information Standards Organization, www.niso.org/apps/group_public/ download.php/13388/rp-19-2014_ODI.pdf.

NISO (2014b) *NISO RP-9-2014 Knowledge Bases and Related Tools (KBART) Recommended Practice*, National Information Standards Organization, www.niso.org/apps/group_public/download.php/ 12720/rp-9-2014_KBART.pdf.

OpenDOAR (2015) *Proportion of Repositories by Country*, www.opendoar.org/onechart.php?cID=&ctID=&rtID=&clID=&lID= &potID=&rSoftWareName=&search=&groupby=c.cCountry&order by=Tally%20DESC&charttype=pie&width=600&height=300&captio n=Proportion%20of%20Repositories%20by%20Country%20- %20Worldwide.

PR Newswire (2013) International Publisher Agreements Expand Summon Discovery Service Content: ProQuest to work with Minha Biblioteca, Universitetsforlaget AS, Boom uitgevers Den Haag, 9 October, www.prnewswire.com/news-releases/ international-publisher-agreements-expand-summon-discovery- service-content-227053641.html.

ProQuest (2015) Delivering a Complete Solution to Research Needs at the University of Murcia, blog, 29 April, http://bit.ly/1mabtMy.

Seeman, D. and Goddard, L. (2014) Preparing the Way: creating future compatible cataloging data in a transitional environment, *Cataloging & Classification Quarterly*, **53** (3/4), 331–40.

Shreeves, S. L., Riley, J. and Milewicz, L. (2006) Moving Towards Shareable Metadata, *First Monday*, **8** (6), http://journals.uic.edu. proxy.mul.missouri.edu/ojs/index.php/fm/article/view/1386.

Somerville, M. M. and Conrad, L. Y. (2014) *Collaborative Improvements in the Discoverability of Scholarly Content: accomplishments, aspirations, and opportunities: a SAGE white paper*, www.sagepub.com/ repository/binaries/pdf/improvementsindiscoverability.pdf.

St Pierre, M. and LaPlant, W. P. (1998) *Issues in Crosswalking Content Metadata Standards*, National Information Standards Organization, www.niso.org/publications/white_papers/crosswalk.

Vaughan, J. (2012) Investigations into Library Web-Scale Discovery Services, *Information Technology and Libraries*, **31** (1), 32–82.

Woodley, M. S. (2008) Crosswalks, Metadata Harvesting, Federated Searching, Metasearching: using metadata to connect users and information. In Baca, M. (ed.), *Introduction to Metadata, Online Edition, Version 3.0*, www.getty.edu/research/publications/ electronic_publications/intrometadata.

Zeng, M. L. and Chan, L. M. (2006) Metadata Interoperability and Standardization: a study of methodology part II: achieving interoperability at the record and repository levels, *D-Lib Magazine*, **12** (6), www.dlib.org/dlib/june06/zeng/06zeng.html.

Zeng, M. L. and Qin, J. (2008) *Metadata*, Neal-Schuman.

Suggested reading

Levine-Clark, M., McDonald, J. and Price, J. (2014) Discovery or Displacement? A large-scale longitudinal study of the effect of discovery systems on online journal usage, *Insights*, **27** (3).

Schonfeld, R. C. (2014) *Does Discovery Still Happen in the Library? Roles and strategies for a shifting reality*, www.sr.ithaka.org/sites/default/ files/files/SR_Briefing_Discovery_20140924_0.pdf.

Notes

1 www.loc.gov/z3950.

2 www.oclc.org/research/themes/data-science/srw.html.

3 See www.exlibrisgroup.com/category/PrimoOverview, www.proquest.com/products-services/The-Summon-Service.html, www.ebscohost.com/discovery and www.oclc.org/worldcat-discovery.en.html.

4 See http://projectblacklight.org and http://vufind-org.github.io/vufind.

5 See www.sirsidynix.com/products/enterprise, www.iii.com/products/sierra/encore and www.bibliocommons.com/products/bibliocore.

6 See http://dublincore.org/documents/dces/.

7 www.exlibrisgroup.com/category/bXRecommender.

8 www.openarchives.org/rs/toc.

9 See www.um.es/web/biblioteca/contenido.

10 See http://nsulib.nsu.ac.kr.

11 See www.unisg.ch/en/wissen/bibliothek/recherche.

12 http://pro.europeana.eu/structure/project-list.

13 www.opendoar.org/search.php.

CHAPTER 3

Managing linked open data across discovery systems

Ali Shiri and Danoosh Davoodi

Introduction

This chapter examines and explores linked open data in the context of the current digital data landscape, drawing on recent developments associated with digital data: big data, research data, open data and web of data. A specific goal of this chapter is to draw attention to the importance of the ways in which linked open data can provide libraries with opportunities to enhance the findability of their data and information resources, and to support seamless and unified access in heterogeneous content repositories, such as digital libraries and integrated discovery systems. The first part of the chapter addresses the key concepts of big data, research data, the Semantic Web and open data. The second part of the chapter focuses on the definition and importance of linked data and its current applications in various settings. Specific examples of libraries and major projects associated with using and implementing linked open data are briefly reviewed. BIBFRAME is reviewed as a popular framework to support the transformation of library data into linked open data. An overview of publishing linked data is presented, along with a reference to useful resources for publishing, browsing and linking linked open data tools.

Big data

The vast volume, variety and complexity of digital data available on the web has resulted in the emergence of what is called 'big data'. Digital libraries, search engines, social media sites, cloud-based computing infrastructures, as well as virtual collaboratories, e-science, e-humanities and e-social-science projects produce massive volumes of data that call for proper management and preservation planning approaches and strategies in order to provide users with effective and efficient data access. Many terms used in the literature refer to, or are associated with, the phenomenon of big data, including 'digital data', 'research data', 'linked data', 'open data', 'web of data' and 'data repositories' (Borgman, 2012; Hodson, 2012; Lyon, 2007; National Science Foundation, 2012). The availability and discourse of these data types presents new research and development opportunities as well as challenges. To provide a coherent and contextualized understanding of big data, one approach would be to place big data in the context of digital libraries, as the latter have been well researched and share a number of similarities with big data. The three key characteristics of big data cited in the literature – volume, variety and velocity – can be construed as characteristics of large, distributed and multi-topic digital libraries. PC Magazine Encyclopedia defines big data as the massive amounts of data that collect over time that are difficult to analyse and handle using common database management tools. Big data includes business transactions, photos, surveillance videos, activity logs, scientific data from sensors, and unstructured text on the web (PC Magazine Encyclopedia, 2015).

More specifically, Lynch stresses the importance of metadata for big data. He notes that one of the key aspects of data stewardship is 'to define and record appropriate metadata – such as experimental parameters and set-up – to allow for data interpretation. This is best done when the data are captured. Indeed, descriptive metadata are often integrated within the experimental design' (Lynch, 2008). What we really witness on the web is the explosion of massive amounts of data (structured, semi-structured or unstructured) in a wide variety of formats, representing various types of activities, areas and disciplines. In order to facilitate the understanding of the complex and multi-faceted notion of big data, a faceted analysis of big data has recently been conducted (Shiri, 2014a), which includes such key facets as data type, environment, people, operations and activities, analytics and metadata.

The international initiative 'Digging into Data Challenge' was formed initially by the National Science Foundation, the National Endowment for the Humanities, the Social Sciences and Humanities Research Council of Canada, and the Joint Information Systems Committee (JISC) in the UK to fund big data projects (IEEE, n.d.). The key goal of this initiative, 'was to address how "big data" changes the research landscape for the humanities and social sciences'. The projects that were funded as part of this initiative include:

- analysis of text and topic
- exploration of full text content of digital historical records
- creation of topic lifecycles across disciplines

- analysis of trends in research disciplines
- analysis of digitized books and databases
- analysis of metadata records in repositories
- creation of new visualization techniques for large-scale linguistic and literary corpora.

A glance at these topics shows the importance of metadata and semantic interoperability in the context of very large data sets in digital libraries and archives, institutional repositories, and digital and cultural heritage information repositories.

Research data

Research data has recently been viewed as being part of a larger data landscape, namely big data. A number of researchers have referred to research data, linked data, the web of data and open data as constituting elements of the big data landscape (Hodson, 2012; Shiri, 2014a). The report of the 2011 Canadian Research Data Summit (Research Data Strategy Working Group, 2011) provides a specific categorization of digital data – research data – produced by academia, industry and government. The sharing of research data has long been a practice among many research communities, often through informal means made increasingly easy with the advent of the internet and associated tools, such as email and ftp sites. Borgman (2007) provides four reasons for sharing research data: 'to (a) reproduce or verify research, (b) make results of publicly funded research available to the public, (c) enable others to ask new questions of extant data, and (d) advance the state of research and innovation'. Borgman notes also that common metadata formats, ontologies and data structures support the integration of multiple data sources and services.

The rise of the open data and open science data movements, in conjunction with the increasing implementation of data management and sharing policies by funding bodies, governments and journals, has led to an explosion in the number of research data services created to serve institutions, association members and research communities. As of May 2015, Databib (http://databib. org/about.php) and re3data.org, now a merged service, maintained a listing of more than 1200 data repositories. Many services enable the deposit of research data and associated metadata, while others focus on metadata describing research data that is housed in other repositories.

A comparative study of metadata practices in four research data repositories – Dryad, FigShare, Dataverse Network and DataCite – showed that there were research data specific metadata elements used by the four research data services examined, and that metadata and semantic interoperability calls for further co-ordination, and for the development of metadata elements for research data (Farnel and Shiri, 2014). Libraries are increasingly viewed as data partners that are in charge of acquiring, managing and making research data accessible in an integrated and meaningful manner. Research data in libraries may reside in various places, depending on the parent institution's policy. Some institutions provide university-wide initiatives and data management plans, while others encourage the use of an institutional repository or are part of a library's holding. Whatever the case, findability, searchability and retrievability of data in a coherent fashion are key considerations for libraries and discovery systems. Data storage, archiving and preservation, metadata standards, technical standards such as file formats, and data sharing and citation are among the key facets of research data management.

Linked open data and web of data

'The term Linked Data refers to a set of best practices for publishing and connecting structured data on the Web. These best practices have been adopted by an increasing number of data providers over the last three years, leading to the creation of a global data space containing billions of assertions – the Web of Data' (Bizer, Heath and Berners-Lee, 2009). It is important to distinguish between the hypertext web and the web of data. Bizer, Heath and Berners-Lee (2009) note that

> while the primary units of the hypertext Web are HTML
> (HyperText Markup Language) documents connected by untyped
> hyperlinks, Linked Data relies on documents containing data in
> Resource Description Framework (RDF) format. However, rather
> than simply connecting these documents, linked data uses RDF to
> make typed statements that link arbitrary things in the world. The
> result, which we will refer to as the Web of Data, may more
> accurately be described as a web of things in the world, described
> by data on the Web.

Linked data principles proposed by Berners-Lee (2006) provide a more specific account of the method for publishing linked data on the web as follows:

- Use uniform resource identifiers (URIs) as names for things.
- Use Hypertext Transfer Protocol (HTTP) URIs so that people can look up those names.
- When someone looks up a URI, provide useful information, using the standards (RDF*, SPARQL).
- Include links to other URIs, so that they can discover more things.

A more technical definition of the term 'linked data' refers to its machine readability, explicit definition of data, and its ability to link or be linked to external data sources (Bizer, Heath and Berners-Lee, 2009). Technically, the term 'linked data' refers to a set of best practices for publishing and connecting structured data on the web in a way that data is machine readable, its meaning is explicitly defined, it is linked to other external datasets, and can in turn be linked to from external datasets (Volz et al., 2009).

The expression of 'web of data' has been widely used in tandem with linked data. The expression points to the emerging data paradigm on the web that is represented as interlinking datasets and sources on the web to support semantically enhanced and meaningfully presented data on the web for searching, browsing, navigation and exploration. The expressions 'web of data', 'Semantic Web' and 'linked data' are interrelated and have been sometimes used interchangeably in the literature. For instance, Bizer, Heath and Berners-Lee (2009) call the Semantic Web: 'a web of data that can be processed directly or indirectly by machines. Therefore, while the Semantic Web, or web of data, is the goal or the end result of this process, Linked Data provides the means to reach that goal.' In one of his presentations, Berners-Lee (2008) referred to the linked open data movement as 'Semantic Web done right'. This implies that Semantic Web and web of data are used as synonymous terms that can be used to promote the creation and use of linked open data in various contexts. Bizer, Heath and Berners-Lee (2009) point to the importance of metadata as a distinguishing factor between web of data and other data fusion scenarios. They note that metadata about published data allows people to assess the quality and trustworthiness of data, and provides opportunities to choose between different means of access. Tim Berners-Lee (2006) notes that:

> The Semantic Web isn't just about putting data on the web. It is
> about making links, so that a person or machine can explore the
> web of data. With linked data, when you have some of it, you can
> find other, related, data. Like the web of hypertext, the web of data
> is constructed with documents on the web. However, unlike the
> web of hypertext, where links are relationships anchors in
> hypertext documents written in HTML, for data they links between
> arbitrary things described by RDF [*sic*].

The notion of the Semantic Web has a longer history than linked
and open data, dating back to 2001, when Berners-Lee envisioned
that content of the world wide web could be further delineated
and structured through coding implementations beyond the basic
display-level functionalities of HTML; automated processes could
then achieve a much higher degree of proficiency in identifying
and merging sources from across the web. In order to facilitate
this transition, Berners-Lee and his associates outlined one of the
first conceptualizations of the notion of the Semantic Web
(Berners-Lee, Hendler and Lassila, 2001).

The purpose of the Semantic Web is to foster a system of
human–computer interaction that affords a much higher order of
information-based task automation involving web content. In
order to achieve this, attention must be temporarily withdrawn
from how human operators view web content, and shifted back
to how computer applications themselves interpret the
information stored in digital documents. The intended
methodology for achieving this is predicated on the future
creation of a secondary digital architecture connected to the web's
current platform of existing content. This architecture would not
only allow application programs to identify successfully
equivalent instances of the same concepts as they occur in

multiple documents, but it would also allow for automated inferential processes to occur independently based on delineated relationships proposed to exist between dissimilar yet connected concepts. Therefore, where the first two iterations of the web may be seen to share the same intended human audience and can be further independently characterized by arguing that the first connects documents and the second connects people, the third iteration will not only once again reassign the primary identity of nodes being linked, but it will also shift the purview of audience towards something that is distinctly non-human. For the Semantic Web, the base audience will become the application programs themselves, while the primary nature of nodes being connected will become the concepts and ideas that are first generated in human understanding and later embodied as various instances in the documents we create. In a recent paper, Calaresu and Shiri (2015) introduce a conceptual model for understanding the Semantic Web. They argue that the early model of the Semantic Web provided a highly abstract and formalized conceptualization for envisioning the Semantic Web, followed by linked data models that focus on materializing and putting into action a workable and pragmatic Semantic Web.

Linked data aims to achieve the goal of the Semantic Web through the provision of a set of standards, data publishing models and methods that bring consistency, interoperability and sharability to unorganized and unidentifiable data on the web. Semantic Web standards introduced in the previous years have now matured and been integrated to support the creation and promotion of linked data. For instance, a quick overview of one of the more prevalent illustrative models of the Semantic Web, known as the Semantic Stack, shows a range of semantic and syntactic technologies and tools necessary for the creation of the

Semantic Web. The common components of these Semantic Stack models include:

- ontologies and taxonomies (OWL)
- mark-up languages and formats: XML, XML namespaces, XHTML, RDF, RDF schema
- query languages such as SPARQL
- language text representation such as Unicode
- user interfaces
- rules: Rule Interchange Format (RIF) and Semantic Web Rule Language (SWRL)
- addressing and identifying: HTTP, URIs, internationalized resource identifiers (IRIs)
- abstract layer: trust and logic.

In short, linked data draws on Semantic Web conceptualizations, technologies, standards and languages. Applying and implementing standards allow for a greater degree of consistency and interoperability among various open data sources.

While 'linked data' and 'linked open data' have sometimes been used interchangeably and synonymously, they are different:

> The label 'Linked Open Data' is widely used, but often to refer to Linked Data in general, rather than to Linked Data that is explicitly published under an open license. Not all Linked Data will be open, and not all Open Data will be linked. Therefore care should be taken to use the appropriate term, depending on the licensing terms of the data in question.
>
> Heath, n.d.

This is particularly important, as digital libraries and archives may have various types of linked data that may or may not be open in relation to licensing, access and rights management. An organization may have multiple linked data sets that are available only to the staff within that organization. In contrast, some academic and public libraries may decide to publish their linked data sets widely on the web to enhance and expand their visibility, searchability and findability. This decision depends on the nature and quality of the data sets held by an organization. For example, DBpedia (Auer et al., 2007) represents a community effort to extract structured information from Wikipedia to make it openly available on the web so that other data sets on the web can be linked to it. In line with the developments associated with the open data movement, concepts starting with 'open' are becoming prevalent, for instance, open government, open science, open data, and so on. We are at a particularly interesting juncture where linking data and opening data as widely and as publicly as possible are becoming the obligation and responsibility of not only libraries, archives and museums, but also government organizations and many different types of industries and institutions.

To contextualize linked data in relation to big data, one can argue that linked data in itself may be viewed as one major type of data in the universe of big data. The main argument here is that the formalized, structured and organized nature of linked data and its specific applications, such as linked controlled vocabularies and knowledge organization systems, have the potential to provide a solid semantic foundation for the classification, representation, visualization and organized presentation of big data (Shiri, 2014b).

It is valid to ask what big data has to do with linked data. Some researchers argue that linked open data is part of the big data landscape. For instance, Hitzler and Janowicz (2013) argue that 'it appears to be uncontroversial that Linked Data is part of the big data landscape. We would even go a bit further and claim that Linked Data is an ideal testbed for researching some key Big Data challenges.'

A comparison of the characteristics of big data and linked data may prove useful as we find ourselves in an increasingly data-rich and data-intensive ecology. Figure 3.1 shows a quick comparison of their characteristics.

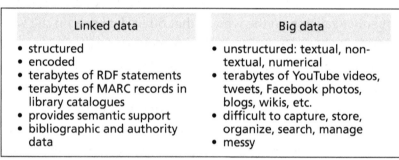

Linked data	Big data
• structured • encoded • terabytes of RDF statements • terabytes of MARC records in library catalogues • provides semantic support • bibliographic and authority data	• unstructured: textual, non-textual, numerical • terabytes of YouTube videos, tweets, Facebook photos, blogs, wikis, etc. • difficult to capture, store, organize, search, manage • messy

Figure 3.1 Comparison of the characteristics of linked data and big data

Linked data is big, but because it is structured and formalized, it can make sense of big data and support its exploration. The Simple Knowledge Organization System (SKOS) standard,[1] developed by the World Wide Web Consortium, aims to build a bridge between the world of knowledge organization systems – including thesauri, classifications, subject headings, taxonomies and folksonomies – and the linked data community, with the goal of bringing benefits to both. SKOS-based linked data controlled vocabularies can provide a semantically rich framework for the analysis and visualization of big data. Leveraging the power of vocabularies and natural language processing for the semantic analysis and visualization of text can be particularly useful.

SKOS-based vocabularies can be used to provide the means for big data analysis and visualization.

The discussion of big data, research data, open and linked data above points to the variety of data sources that libraries and information agencies gather, organize and aim to make available as part of their integrated discovery systems. Taking a holistic approach to data and information with discovery systems is crucially important as an increasing number of libraries acquire various types of data and have the responsibility of organizing it, and making it accessible in a seamless manner.

Linked open data in libraries

The promise of linked open data on the web has made libraries rethink the ways in which they create and manage information:

> I would wager that we are seeing the end of the 'pure' library cataloging record that contains only library-provided data. The future will be about data more than records, and the data will come from heterogeneous sources. This requires us to be more thorough in our data definitions, but also to design data knowing that it will have uses independent of a single, controlling record.
>
> Coyle, 2009

Coyle points to the flexibility and wider applicability of data in the context of libraries, which for decades have been using encoding and cataloguing systems to organize bibliographic data. The bibliographic data models have evolved through time to accommodate the need for more up-to-date digital materials, as well as to provide better search and discovery services. One of the main challenges of integrating bibliographic data in the

Semantic Web environment lies in the way the data is encoded.

Machine-Readable Cataloging (MARC) is one the most popular standards that was developed for the purpose of creating and sharing library materials in a way that can be used and read by computers. The model was developed in the 1960s and has been an international standard since 1973. The MARC record format was designed decades before the advent of the web. The recent surge of interest in the Semantic Web and open linked data has made the evaluation of MARC as a bibliographic system necessary. Developed for the exchange of bibliographic records between mainframe computers in times when storage and bandwidth were extremely scarce commodities, MARC was optimized to squeeze data into the smallest possible package, encoded using conventions that are not flexible enough today. The MARC model for representing library items is somewhat flat, and makes the creation of relationships between and among entities cumbersome and hard to understand. As was mentioned earlier, however, defining the relationship among entities is a fundamental building block of the web. As a result of this demand, library and information science researchers and practitioners have been exploring and developing models that can transform the MARC metadata scheme into an entity-relationship model that is more conducive to machine processing and has the ability to leverage the existing web environment to give libraries greater visibility, and to take advantage of the robust technology that the web has developed.

Semantic Web technologies conceptualize data in a way that fundamentally differs from the conceptualization underlying the data formats of the 20th century. Linked data is primarily about meaning and meaningful relationships between things, while traditional library data formats combine the meaning of data and the structured encoding of data into a single package. In order to bring the vast body of library bibliographic content to the Semantic Web, it is necessary to transform the lower-level transport structures as well as the conventions used to express data elements. The recent revision of the Anglo-American Cataloguing Rules (AACR2) to Resource Description and Access (RDA) was intended to bring cataloguing practices into a form more consistent with the Semantic Web. The AACR2 was a set of cataloguing rules that had been developed since the 1960s. The AARC2 was not flexible to accommodate the organization of materials in the digital data landscape. The RDA standard is flexible for cataloguing and resource description of all kinds of physical and digital materials, and meets the resource description and discovery needs of the new digital environment. Based on the Functional Requirements for Bibliographic Records (FRBR), the RDA standard supports users in finding, selecting, identifying and obtaining information resources.

The linked data approach offers significant advantages over current practices for creating and delivering library data, and provides a natural extension to the collaborative sharing models historically employed by libraries. Linked data, especially linked open data, is sharable, extensible and easily re-usable. With linked open data, libraries can increase their presence on the web, where most information seekers can be found. Linked data supports multilingual functionality for data and user services, such as the labelling of concepts identified by language-agnostic URIs. These characteristics are inherent in the linked data standards, and are supported by the use of web-friendly identifiers for data and concepts. Therefore libraries will be able to create an open, global pool of shared data that can be used and re-used to describe resources, with a limited amount of redundant effort, compared with current cataloguing processes. In summary, presenting library resources and data using linked data principles can:

- make it easier to search for and locate the library resources on the web
- allow for invention of more creative applications on the web based on library resources
- provide opportunities for cataloguing efficiency and innovations.

One of the key challenges of the current digital data landscape is interoperability. For decades, libraries have explored the ways in which semantic, subject and technical interoperability can be achieved through following various standards. Given the variety, diversity and heterogeneity of data sources on the web, the notion of library metadata interoperability in an open data environment is particularly important. Dunsire, Hillmann and Phipps (2012) note how the meaning and implications of mapping can change:

> The meaning and implications of 'mapping' changes radically when moving from a database and record-based approach to an open, multi-domain, global, shared environment based on linked data technologies – where anybody can say anything about any topic, validity constraints are not acknowledged, a nearly infinite number of properties can be defined to describe an infinite number of entities, and authority is multidimensional and often ephemeral. The classic approach to such apparent chaos is to attempt tighter control over the creation process, more filtering, additional restrictions, and less access. This approach hinders appreciation and use of the broad diversity of perspective that comes with a world of open data.

Achieving interoperability within and across libraries in a linked open data web environment poses a new set of challenges and opportunities. Whether it be semantic interoperability, structural interoperability or format interoperability, libraries need a holistic and integrated strategy to achieve interoperability as an instrumental approach to the design of discovery and integrated search systems that provide seamless and inclusive access to data and information.

Linked open data leading projects

In this section we briefly review some of the leading projects that have addressed the transformation of traditional library catalogue data into linked open data.

OCLC

OCLC (the Online Computer Library Center) is among the leaders in applying linked data principles to WorldCat, its large catalogue (OCLC, 2015). OCLC operates as a non-profit membership organization with a wide variety of products and services, and conducts research and development projects. Several OCLC initiatives involve offering OCLC resources as linked data. Some of the main OCLC resources that have been released as linked data include:

- the Virtual International Authority File (VIAF)
- FAST (Faceted Application of Subject Terminology)
- the Dewey Decimal Classification System.

OCLC has been working on new ways of creating linked data as part of the WorldCat metadata repository. WorldCat makes use of Schema.org vocabularies, a method for providing structured data within the web. The presentation of these pages, as seen through web browsers, remains unchanged. The source coding of the page reveals the RDF section to humans, which would also be accessible through software tools designed to operate in the Semantic Web environment (Figure 3.2). All metadata records in WorldCat now include an embedded section that presents the same content in RDF and OWL (Figure 3.3). Although this is currently mostly a proof-of-concept effort, the layering of Schema.org into WorldCat records can be seen as at least a small step in bringing the Semantic Web to libraries.

Each WorldCat record that has been presented in the linked data format can be viewed as an RDF document. While not yet at the point of operationalizing its services through Semantic Web technologies, OCLC stands as one of the few library organizations that is at least making experimental forays into this territory.

The Library of Congress

The Library of Congress is considered a pioneer in experimenting with ways to make cataloguing and metadata record creation more efficient. In 2011, the Library of Congress announced that careful attention would be paid to Semantic Web technologies and linked data principles, with RDF as the basic data model (Marcum, 2011). Progress on many fronts of library technologies demands the transition from MARC to Semantic Web-based standards and technologies. One of the seminal efforts to replace MARC 21 has been launched by the Library of Congress through its Bibliographic Framework Transition Initiative. This project involves mapping all the elements of MARC 21 into a linked data

```
⊟ Linked Data

More info about Linked Data

Primary Entity
<http://www.worldcat.org/oclc/57193246> # Twilight
  a schema:Book, schema:CreativeWork ;
  library:oclcnum "57193246" ;
  library:placeOfPublication <http://id.loc.gov/vocabulary/countries/nyu> ;
  rdfs:comment "Unknown 'gen' value: shs" ;
  schema:about <http://experiment.worldcat.org/entity/work/data/46226229#Topic/verlieben> ; # Verlieben
  schema:about <http://experiment.worldcat.org/entity/work/data/46226229#Topic/wohnungswechsel> ; # Wohnungswechsel
  schema:about <http://experiment.worldcat.org/entity/work/data/46226229#Topic/vampires_fiction> ; # Vampires--Fiction
  schema:about <http://experiment.worldcat.org/entity/work/data/46226229#Place/washington_state> ; # Washington (State)
  schema:about <http://id.worldcat.org/fast/1204703> ; # Washington (State)
  schema:about <http://experiment.worldcat.org/entity/work/data/46226229#Topic/high_schools_fiction> ; # High Schools-Fiction
  schema:about <http://experiment.worldcat.org/entity/work/data/46226229#Topic/tochter> ; # Tochter
  schema:about <http://experiment.worldcat.org/entity/work/data/46226229#Topic/school_stories> ; # School stories
  schema:about <http://experiment.worldcat.org/entity/work/data/46226229#Topic/schools_fiction> ; # Schools-Fiction
  schema:about <http://experiment.worldcat.org/entity/work/data/46226229#Topic/gefahr> ; # Gefahr
  schema:about <http://id.worldcat.org/fast/1163968> ; # Vampires
  schema:about <http://experiment.worldcat.org/entity/work/data/46226229#Topic/vampir> ; # Vampir
  schema:about <http://experiment.worldcat.org/entity/work/data/46226229#Topic/aussenseiterin> ; # Außenseiterin
  schema:about <http://id.worldcat.org/fast/956288> ; # High schools
  schema:about <http://experiment.worldcat.org/entity/work/data/46226229#Topic/high_school> ; # High school
  schema:about <http://experiment.worldcat.org/entity/work/data/46226229#Topic/vater> ; # Vater
  schema:about <http://id.worldcat.org/fast/1107958> ; # Schools
  schema:about <http://experiment.worldcat.org/entity/work/data/46226229#Topic/washington_state_fiction> ; # Washington(Stat
  schema:about <http://experiment.worldcat.org/entity/work/data/46226229#Topic/weibliche_jugend> ; # Weibliche Jugend
  schema:bookEdition "1st ed." ;
  schema:bookFormat bgn:PrintBook ;
  schema:contentRating "720" ;
  schema:copyrightYear "2005" ;
  schema:creator <http://viaf.org/viaf/102313919> ; # Stephenie Meyer
  schema:datePublished "2005" ;
  schema:description "First sight -- Open book -- Phenomenon -- Invitations -- Blood type -- Scary stories -- Nightmare -- Port An
```

Figure 3.2 WorldCat linked data record for the book *Twilight*

```
- <rdf:RDF>
  - <rdf:Description rdf:about="http://id.worldcat.org/fast/956288">
      <rdf:type rdf:resource="http://schema.org/Intangible"/>
      <schema:name xml:lang="en">High schools</schema:name>
    </rdf:Description>
  - <rdf:Description rdf:about="http://experiment.worldcat.org/entity/work/data/46226229#Series/twilight_saga">
      <rdf:type rdf:resource="http://bibliograph.net/PublicationSeries"/>
      <schema:hasPart rdf:resource="http://www.worldcat.org/oclc/57193246"/>
      <schema:name>Twilight Saga ;</schema:name>
      <schema:creator rdf:resource="http://experiment.worldcat.org/entity/work/data/46226229#Person/meyer_stephenie_1973"/>
      <schema:name>Twilight saga ;</schema:name>
    </rdf:Description>
  - <rdf:Description rdf:about="http://experiment.worldcat.org/entity/work/data/46226229#Topic/high_schools_fiction">
      <rdf:type rdf:resource="http://schema.org/Intangible"/>
      <schema:name xml:lang="en">High Schools-Fiction</schema:name>
    </rdf:Description>
  - <rdf:Description rdf:about="http://experiment.worldcat.org/entity/work/data/46226229#Topic/tochter">
      <rdf:type rdf:resource="http://schema.org/Intangible"/>
      <schema:name xml:lang="en">Tochter</schema:name>
    </rdf:Description>
  - <rdf:Description rdf:about="http://experiment.worldcat.org/entity/work/data/46226229#Topic/school_stories">
      <rdf:type rdf:resource="http://schema.org/Intangible"/>
      <schema:name xml:lang="en">School stories</schema:name>
    </rdf:Description>
  - <rdf:Description rdf:about="http://experiment.worldcat.org/entity/work/data/46226229#Topic/aussenseiterin">
      <rdf:type rdf:resource="http://schema.org/Intangible"/>
```

Figure 3.3 WorldCat RDF/XML record for the book *Twilight*

structure. The proposed mappings, vocabularies and general discussion of the project have been made publicly available through the BIBFRAME.org website. In addition to the BIBFRAME, the Library of Congress provides a linked data service for its authorities and vocabularies (http://id.loc.gov). The service provides access and search functionality to commonly found standards and vocabularies promulgated by the Library of Congress. This includes data values and the controlled vocabularies that house them. These are some of the Library of Congress's available datasets:

- LC Subject Headings
- LC Name Authority File
- LC Classification
- LC Children's Subject Headings
- LC Genre/Form Terms
- LC Medium of Performance Thesaurus for Music
- Thesaurus for Graphic Materials
- Cultural Heritage Organizations
- MARC countries
- MARC Geographic Areas
- MARC Languages
- identifiers
- carriers
- content types
- media types.

The German National Library

The German National Library has created a linked data service through which it has been supplying its data in the RDF standard via the linked data service since 2010. The service uses the entire national bibliography data to present and link records. Records in the catalogue are available in MARC 21-XML, RDF/XML and the newly introduced BIBFRAME (Deutsche National Bibliotek, n.d.).

The British Library

The British Library has been actively involved in developing linked data compatible bibliographic resources (British Library, n.d.). It has developed a linked data version of the British National Bibliography (BNB) available as linked open data. The Library provides SPARQL editor and endpoint services, and has linked its data to other datasets in the linked open data cloud, including Library of Congress Subject Headings (LCSH), VIAF, Lexvo, GeoNames, MARC country, RDF Book Mashup and Dewey.info. Data is described using properties from the following vocabularies:

- Bibliographic Ontology
- Bio: A Vocabulary for Biographical Information
- British Library Terms
- Dublin Core
- Event Ontology
- FOAF: Friend of a Friend
- ISBD
- Org: An Organization Ontology
- OWL
- SKOS
- RDF schema
- WGS84 Geo Positioning.

The Bibliothèque nationale de France

The Bibliothèque nationale de France (BnF), the National Library of France, provides a data service that grants access to its library data in RDF/XML, RDF/N3, RDF/NT and JavaScript Object Notation (JSON) formats (BnF, n.d.). The data is automatically gathered and generated from existing data in formats such as InterMarc for the main catalogue, XML-EAD for archives inventories, and Dublin Core for the digital library. The data in the BnF data service can be displayed as RDF linked open data, and is available for all records in the entire database. Additionally, it can be queried through a SPARQL endpoint. The BnF data service has linked its data to the VIAF, the International Standard Name Identifier (ISNI), the authority repository of the higher education libraries (IdRef) and DBpedia. Table 3.1 shows examples of linked data sets available and their description.

Table 3.1 Linked open data sets	
Dataset	**Description**
Library of Congress Name Authority File	Bulk downloads of the Library of Congress Name Authority File. The current bulk download is only MADS/RDF. A SKOS/RDF download will be available in the near future. Two serializations are offered: n-triples and RDF/XML.
LCSubjects.org LCSH	An alternative to http://id.loc.gov/: includes a SPARQL endpoint, faceted search.
data.bnf.fr – BnF	data.bnf.fr gathers data from the different databases of the BnF, to create web pages about works, authors, subjects and places together with a RDF view on the extracted data.
datos.bne.es	Open bibliographic linked data from the Spanish National Library including 4 million authority records and 2.4 million bibliographic records resulting in over 58 million triples. A triple defines a directed binary relation between two resources: the binary relation is called a *predicate* or a *property*; the two resources are *subject* and *object*. These three elements form a *triple* and they are all identified by URIs, e.g., The Mona Lisa (subject) was created by (predicate) Leonardo da Vinci (object).

Table 3.1 (Continued)

Dataset	Description
Deutsche Nationalbibliografie (DNB)	The Linked Data Service of the German National Library has expanded and includes bibliographic data since January 2012. As a first step, the bibliographic data of the DNB's main collection (apart from the printed music and the collection of the Deutsches Exilarchiv) and the serials (magazines, newspapers and series of the German Union Catalogue of serials – Zeitschriftendatenbank or ZDB) has been converted.
AGROVOC	The AGROVOC thesaurus is a multilingual, terminological backbone for agricultural digital goods.
Hungarian National Library (NSZL) catalogue	OPAC and Digital Library and the corresponding authority data as linked open data.
BibBase	Facilitates the dissemination of scientific publications over the internet. BibBase makes it easy for scientists to maintain their publications pages. Scientists simply maintain a bibtex file of their publications, including links to the papers, and BibBase does the rest. When a web user visits your publications page, BibBase dynamically generates an always up-to-date HTML page from the bibtex file.
MedLine	RDF representation of the MedLine catalogue. Information about 19 million articles linked to http://dx.doi.org/ with article identifiers and http://crossref.org/ with journal identifiers.
BNB	BNB published as Linked Data by the British Library, linked to external sources including VIAF, LCSH, Lexvo, GeoNames, MARC country and language, Dewey.info and RDF Book Mashup. Published to this data model for books and this data model for serials.
Cambridge University Library	Marks the first major output of the COMET (Cambridge Open Metadata) project, a JISC funded collaboration between Cambridge University Library and Centre for Applied Research in Educational Technologies, University of Cambridge. It represents work over a 20+ year period, which contains a number of changes in practices and cataloguing tools.
Europeana linked open data	Contains open metadata on 2.4 million texts, images, videos and sounds gathered by Europeana. These objects come from data providers that have reacted early and positively to Europeana's initiative of promoting more open data and new data exchange agreements.
LIBRIS	Swedish Union Catalogue, Swedish National Bibliography and authority data. The National Bibliography and authority data is part of Libris, the Swedish Union Catalogue, and the long term goal is to release the whole database under an open licence. The data contains links to Wikipedia, DBpedia, LC authorities (names and subjects) and VIAF.
Princeton Library Finding Aids	Explore descriptions of unique holdings at the Princeton University Libraries, which include manuscripts, archival collections, images, ephemera, and much more one-of-a-kind material.

Tools, techniques, and procedures for library linked open data

Libraries are experiencing a time of huge, tumultuous change. The Library Linked Data Incubator Group (a W3C working group) final report states that library data is not integrated with the web, much of it is encoded in natural language rather than as data, library standards serve only the library community and no other, and changes in library technology are often completely dependent on the expertise of vendors (Baker et al., 2011). There has been increasing pressure either to adapt standards that have been in use for decades to new circumstances, or to replace them with different standards. It is clear that change is happening, but the trajectory of this change is less clear. If MARC and AACR2 are no longer to be used as encoding and cataloguing standards, what standards should serve? One possible path forward is provided by the standards established by the World Wide Web Consortium to build the Semantic Web. Linked data, in particular, is an implementation of these standards that seems to fit well with the legacy metadata produced and maintained by libraries.

Library data in linked data format (MARC to RDF)

One can describe objects using RDF/XML or any other type of RDF schema. As was mentioned earlier, RDF schema or other vocabularies identify and control the type of relationship between entities. These vocabularies are not designed to represent library specific data, therefore some rich features of bibliographic description models (e.g., FRBR) cannot be accurately described; for example OCLC uses schema.org. An examination of schema.org shows that it falls short in describing the domain of library resources and services. For instance, it does not address the FRBR, which is the basis for the RDA standard. There is no clear distinction between content and carrier. Very few relationships among creative works have been defined. There is no concept of collection or series. And there are no models of transactions involving library resources and the organizations that provide or receive them, such as libraries, universities, publishers, e-content aggregators and data service providers. These shortcomings push the library community to think of a new model for transforming data from MARC to the linked data platform.

BIBFRAME

The Bibliographic Framework (BIBFRAME) was initiated by the Library of Congress in 2011 as a framework model to describe the transition from MARC to linked data platform (Library of Congress, n.d.). It is the foundation for the future of bibliographic description that exists in the web and the networked world in which we live. The model is designed to deal with older and new records. In short, the BIBFRAME model serves the purpose of data migration from standalone library catalogues to a large, global and interconnected database, formally known as the 'web of data'. Miller et al. (2012) mention the following factors that BIBFRAME attempts to balance:

- flexibility to accommodate future cataloguing domains, and entirely new use scenarios and sources of information
- the web as an architectural model for expressing and connecting decentralized information
- social and technical adoption outside the library community
- social and technical deployment within the library community

- previous efforts in expressing bibliographic material as linked data
- the application of machine technology for mechanical tasks while amply accommodating the subject matter expert (the librarian) as the explicit brain behind the mechanics
- previous efforts for modelling bibliographic information in the library publishing, archival and museum communities
- the robust and beneficial history and aspects of a common method of bibliographic information transfer.

In translating the MARC 21 format to a linked data model, BIBFRAME deconstructs the MARC record into the following classes:

- *creative work*: a resource reflecting a conceptual essence of the cataloguing resource
- *instance*: a resource reflecting an individual, material embodiment of the work
- *authority*: a resource reflecting key authority concepts that have defined relationships reflected in the work and instance (e.g., people, places, topics and organizations); one important concept in authority is domain, which is the entity responsible for the recognition, organization and maintenance (to ensure integrity) of the authoritative resources
- *annotation*: a resource that enhances our knowledge about another resource when knowing, minimally, 'who' is doing the annotating is important; library holdings, cover art and reviews are examples types.

The BIBFRAME model uses entity-relationship models and

includes FRBR concepts. The model recognizes entities, attributes and relationships between entities, which is the main concept of the RDF standard. BIBFRAME thus uses the RDF modelling practice of uniquely identifying as web resources all entities (resources), attributes and relationships between entities (properties). This allows for further annotations (such as mappings to other vocabularies or local community extensions) to be enabled as needed. These information resources can then be reconstructed into a single coherent architecture that allows for co-operative cataloguing at a far more granular level than before. This model is far more compatible with linked data model requirements than the MARC model. Through the BIBFRAME model, every record can be presented in pieces of data that can be linked, shared and re-used. Further, these information assets can now be used more effectively at a granular level, and can provide a richer substrate in which local collections, special collections and third-party data can easily be annotated and contextualized in a co-operative library content.

Changes to the foundational underpinnings, such as the MARC formats, will have major ramifications on many aspects of library automation. At a minimum, systems reliant on MARC will need to accommodate new formats, such as those that may ultimately emerge from the BIBFRAME model. Beyond the adjustment of legacy products to support new formats, more substantial benefits will accrue to those products and services that fully exploit the full potential of the Semantic Web and open linked data. A mapping of MARC 21 to RDF can be found at MARC Must Die (2010).

Publishing linked data
By publishing data on the web according to the linked data

principles, data providers add their data to a global data space, which allows data to be discovered and used by various applications. Publishing a data set as linked data on the web involves the following three basic steps:

- Assign URIs to the entities described by the data set and provide for dereferencing these URIs over the HTTP protocol into RDF representations.
- Set RDF links to other data sources on the web, so that clients can navigate the web of data as a whole by following RDF links.
- Provide metadata about published data, so that clients can assess the quality of published data and choose between different means of access.

A variety of linked data publishing tools has been developed, which either serve the content of RDF stores as linked data on the web, or provide linked data views over non-RDF legacy data sources. These tools allow publishers to avoid dealing with technical details such as content negotiation, to ensure that data is published according to the linked data community best practices (Berrueta et al., 2008; Sauermann, Cyganiak and Völkel, 2011). All tools support dereferencing URIs into RDF descriptions. In addition, some of these tools provide SPARQL query access to the already available datasets, and support the publication of RDF dumps. There are many linked data browsers, mashups and client applications that libraries and information services may want to use. The World Wide Web Consortium provides useful resources for these tools and applications (Heath, n.d.); these include linked data publishing platforms and frameworks, linked data and RDF editors and validators, tools for consuming linked data, and linked data applications for end-users.

Libraries can also take advantage of linked data technology in representing their resources on the web and enhancing the user online visit to the libraries. Linked data browsing tools (server-side and client-side) can be used on library websites and applications to provide more accurate search and recovery of data for the user, not only from the library's local database, but from data linkage to other libraries' datasets around the world. Additionally, creative mashups of library data with other datasets (location, social, etc.) can enrich user experience and use valuable library data in settings other than what they have been using so far.

Conclusion and recommendations

It is evident that with the explosion of a variety of datasets available on the web, libraries and information services need to apply standards to ensure the effective management, accessibility and retrieval of data. As was stated in the earlier part of this chapter, there are new and emerging concurrent trends in regard to data on the web, including open data, big data and research data, which challenge libraries and information services, as well as any information handling organizations. Linked open data provides standards, tools and applications that can support various data sets, and allow libraries to leverage effectively the power of their legacy bibliographic surrogates, as well as modern metadata repositories. Libraries must develop holistic strategies to ensure that access to data and information in their collections follows a coherent description and encoding model to support uniform searching, browsing and exploration across heterogeneous information and data sources.

A major advantage of linked data technology in this context is that it allows for establishing connections between and across various datasets. In the library world, achieving these connections will be key to success. As was noted earlier, many semantically annotated links have been created between published value vocabularies in the linked data clouds. This is a great achievement for the first steps in building the library linked data community. This is just the beginning, however, and much more needs be done to resolve the problem of redundancy among the various authority resources maintained by large numbers of libraries. More links are also needed among datasets and among the metadata element sets used to structure linked data descriptions. Depending on the nature and suitability of datasets, libraries can be selective about which linked data sources would be of value to their own communities. Libraries should embrace the web of data, both by making their data available for use as linked data, and by using the web of data in their discovery systems and search services. Ideally, library data should integrate fully with other resources on the web, creating greater visibility for libraries, and ensuring that rich discovery and access services are available to information seekers. With their long standing tradition of creating and managing valuable structures, libraries have a unique opportunity to take on a leadership role in the provision of seamless and coherent access to data and information sources for their own communities and the global community of web users.

Tools and frameworks reviewed briefly in this chapter may serve different functions for different types of libraries and information services. Frameworks such as BIBFRAME provide guidelines that support the transformation of library data into linked open data that can enrich and enhance information and data services offered by libraries. Linked data is a global approach towards realizing the long envisioned Semantic Web. Libraries with semantically enhanced and rich collections can serve as major building blocks for realizing this vision. If Semantic Web standards do not fully support the translation of library data with sufficient expressivity, there is an opportunity for libraries to expand and extend existing standards further to make them more relevant and useful. This is similar to what some frameworks are doing for linked data standards.

References

Auer, S., Bizer, C., Kobilarov, G., Lehmann, J., Cyganiak, R. and Ives, Z. (2007) *Dbpedia: a nucleus for a web of open data*, Springer.

Baker, T., Bermès, E., Coyle, K., Dunsire, G., Isaac, A., Murray, P., Panzer, P., Schneider, J., Singer, R., Summers, E., Waites, W., Young, J. and Zheng, M. (2011) *Library Linked Data Incubator Group Final Report*, W3C, www.w3.org/2005/Incubator/lld/XGR-lld-20111025.

Berners-Lee, T. (2006) *Design Issues: linked data*, www.w3.org/DesignIssues/LinkedData.html.

Berners-Lee, T. (2008) *Linked Open Data*, www.w3.org/2008/Talks/0617-lod-tbl/#%281%29.

Berners-Lee, T., Hendler, J. and Lassila, O. (2001) *The Semantic Web*, http://www.krchowdhary.com/ai/ai16/sematic%20web-sci-am.pdf.

Berrueta, D., Phipps, J., Miles, A., Baker, T. and Swick, R. (2008) *Best Practice Recipes for Publishing RDF Vocabularies*, W3C, www.w3.org/TR/swbp-vocab-pub/.

Bizer, C., Heath, T. and Berners-Lee, T. (2009) Linked Data: the story so far. In Sheth, A. (ed.), *Semantic Services, Interoperability and Web Applications: emerging concepts*, IGI Global.

BnF (n.d.) Welcome to data.bnf.fr, Bibliothèque nationale de France, http://data.bnf.fr.

Borgman, C. (2007) *Scholarship in the Digital Age: information, infrastructure, and the internet*, MIT Press.

Borgman, C. L. (2012) The Conundrum of Sharing Research Data, *Journal of the American Society for Information Science and Technology*, **63** (6), 1059–78.

British Library (n.d.) The British National Bibliography as Linked Open Data, http://bnb.data.bl.uk/.

Calaresu, M. and Shiri, A. (2015) Understanding Semantic Web: a conceptual model, *Library Review*, **64** (1/2), 82–100.

Coyle, K. (2009) Metadata Mix and Match, *Information Standards Quarterly*, **21** (1), 9–11, http://kcoyle.net/isqv21no1.pdf.

Deutsche National Bibliotek (n.d.) Linked Data Service of the German National Library, www.dnb.de/EN/Service/DigitaleDienste/ LinkedData/linkeddata_node.html.

Dunsire, G., Hillmann, D. and Phipps, J. (2012) Reconsidering Universal Bibliographic Control in Light of the Semantic Web, *Journal of Library Metadata*, **12** (2–3), 164–76.

Farnel, S. and Shiri, A. (2014) Metadata for Research Data. In *Proceedings of the International Conference on Dublin Core and Metadata Applications*, Austin, Texas, USA, http://dcevents.dublincore.org/IntConf/dc-2014/paper/view/236.

Heath, T. (n.d.) *Linked Data: connect distributed data across the web: frequently asked questions*, http://linkeddata.org/faq.

Hitzler, P. and Janowicz, K. (2013) Linked Data, Big Data, and the 4th Paradigm, *Semantic Web*, **4** (3), 233–5.

Hodson, S. (2012) JISC and Big Data. In *Eduserv Symposium 2012: big data, big deal?*, London.

IEEE (n.d.) *Digging into Data Challenge*, Institute of Electrical and Electronics Engineers, http://diggingintodata.org.

Library of Congress (n.d.) Bibliographic Framework Initiative, www.loc.gov/bibframe.

Lynch, C. (2008) Big Data: how do your data grow?, *Nature*, **455**, 4 September, 28–9, www.nature.com/nature/journal/v455/n7209/

full/455028a.html.

Lyon, L. (2007) *Dealing with Data: roles, rights, responsibilities and relationships, consultancy report,*
www.jisc.ac.uk/media/documents/programmes/digitalrepositories/
dealing_with_data_report-final.pdf.

MARC Must Die (2010) MARC to RDF Mapping: MARC 21 format for bibliographic data to RDF mapping, http://marc-must-die.info/
index.php/MARC_to_RDF_mapping.

Marcum, D. (2011) *A Bibliographic Framework for the Digital Age,*
www.loc.gov/bibframe/news/framework-103111.html.

Miller, E., Ogbuji, U., Mueller, V. and MacDougall, K. (2012)
Bibliographic Framework as a Web of Data: linked data model and supporting services, https://www.loc.gov/bibframe/pdf/marcld-
report-11-21-2012.pdf.

National Science Foundation (2012) *Core Techniques and Technologies for Advancing Big Data Science and Engineering (BIGDATA) Solicitation,*
www.nsf.gov/pubs/2012/nsf12499/nsf12499.htm.

OCLC (2015) *Data Strategy and Linked Data: helping libraries thrive on the web,* Online Computer Library Center, www.oclc.org/data.en.html.

PC Magazine Encyclopedia (2015) *Big Data,*
www.pcmag.com/encyclopedia/term/62849/big-data.

Research Data Strategy Working Group (2011) *Mapping the Data Landscape: report of the 2011 Canadian Research Data Summit,*
www.rdc-drc.ca/wp-content/uploads/Report-of-the-Canadian-
Research-Data-Summit1.pdf.

Sauermann, L., Cyganiak, R. and Völkel, M. (2011) *Cool URIs for the Semantic Web,* http://scidok.sulb.uni-saarland.de/volltexte/2011/
3944/pdf/TM_07_01.pdf.

Shiri, A. (2014a) Making Sense of Big Data: a facet analysis approach,
Knowledge Organization, **41** (5), 357–68.

Shiri, A. (2014b) Linked Data Meets Big Data: a knowledge

organization systems perspective, *Advances in Classification Research Online*, **24** (1), http://journals.lib.washington.edu/index.php/acro/article/view/14672.

Volz, J., Bizer, C., Gaedke, M. and Kobilarov, G. (2009) *Discovering and Maintaining Links on the Web of Data*, Springer.

Note

1   www.w3.org/2004/02/skos/.

CHAPTER 4

Redefining library resources in discovery systems

Christine DeZelar-Tiedman

Introduction

As the nature and form of the library catalogue has evolved over time, so has the definition of library resources. In fact, the term 'resources' used in this context is a relatively recent development, as traditionally library assets have been referred to as 'materials'. While the word 'materials' is broader in scope than terms for specific things managed by libraries, such as books, journals or DVDs, it still implies a physicality that no longer accurately reflects the wide array of resources managed by libraries, particularly research libraries. Most large research libraries, and many smaller libraries, especially those associated with more recently established academic institutions, allocate a significant proportion of their budgets towards licensed electronic content, including e-books and journals. These resources not only lack a physical embodiment, but they are often not even owned by the library. The library pays for access to the content, but the access is typically not perpetual and can change over time.

The increased scope of web-scale library discovery systems leads us to further reconsider the definition of library resources, and what we provide access to in the catalogue. Along with all the physical and electronic resources managed by the library, additional content provided by users or third parties can be made accessible, as well as a multitude of other services. Should libraries include information about these services within the discovery system? What are the best methods for doing this, and what challenges does this present for the management of metadata?

From catalogue to discovery system

The original library catalogues took several different forms, beginning as books and scrolls inventorying the contents of an individual library's physical collection. These evolved into the nearly ubiquitous card catalogue, which was the primary format from the late 19th century through the 1970s. It is probably safe to say that when online public access catalogues began to emerge in the 1980s, most librarians did not anticipate the multitude of ways in which the continuing development of information technology would force them to completely rethink the role and purpose of the library catalogue. Initially, OPACs sought to replicate as much as possible the features of the card catalogue, in providing an inventory of materials physically held by the library, and allowing users to search by browsing indexes of authors, titles and subjects.

The advent of the world wide web in the early 1990s had an enormous impact on library operations, just as it did on so many aspects of the greater culture. It became *de rigueur* for libraries to create a web page providing information such as building hours, services and staff contact information. The relationship between the library web page and the catalogue was somewhat disjointed:

usually there was a link to the catalogue from the home page, but there was little or no integration of the two. This tension became more pronounced with the emergence of electronic journals. While debate on the cataloguing side of library operations centred on whether to create separate records for electronic journals or use combined print and electronic records, and whether and how to catalogue individual web sites, public services staff took matters into their own hands, and created A–Z lists of electronic journal titles, and library guides highlighting recommended websites for particular subject areas. Some cataloguers felt threatened that the centrality of the catalogue for access to library resources was losing ground, and argued that 'everything should be in the catalogue'. As aggregators of electronic content grew, however, the impracticality of individually cataloguing and maintaining access to packages of hundreds or thousands of electronic resources became apparent.

In the early 2000s, the concept of Web 2.0 began to take prominence, and had a significant impact on the design of library catalogues. Web 2.0 refers to web design that is more social and interactive than earlier websites, often incorporating user-contributed content, such as reviews, tagging and the generation of folksonomies or word clouds, consisting of terms supplied or endorsed by end-users as being relevant or useful in labelling or navigating the site's content. The perception was that library catalogues were losing traffic to commercial sites such as Google and Amazon, which provided more user-friendly interfaces and more satisfactory results, and in the case of Amazon, more interactivity.

The first library catalogue employing Web 2.0 principles to gain wide attention was the Endeca catalogue[1] implemented by North Carolina State University (NCSU) in 2006. Notably, rather than working with a vendor traditionally in the library market, NCSU purchased and modified software used in the retail industry for online shopping. With Endeca, many librarians for the first time encountered a catalogue that included features common on commercial sites, such as images of library resources, faceted browsing of materials by category, improved search speed, results sorted by relevancy ranking, and spell-check, autocorrect and 'did you mean?' prompts as the user was typing in a search query.

As use of Endeca and similar products spread and users responded positively, library vendors began developing catalogue products based on Web 2.0 principles. One area of development that initially garnered much enthusiasm, and some concern, was the ability to provide interactive features, and a platform for user-contributed content. While libraries thought the ability to tag, write reviews, and have online discussions of library materials within the catalogue might draw users, some became concerned with the need to moderate user contributions. Would reviews need to be screened for appropriate content? What if users contributed inaccurate or misleading information? In reality, most of these concerns proved to be unfounded, as libraries discovered that many of the interactive features were little used. While features that helped users with their research tasks, such as creating sets or lists of materials they wished to consult, were popular, most users had little interest in reviewing or tagging in a local library system. Social interaction was more likely to happen in places with a higher aggregation of users (Amazon, Goodreads, Flickr), or in highly specialized communities where there was a perceived return on contributions (Smith-Yoshimura, 2012).

In parallel with Web 2.0 catalogues, development of other types of library repositories began to emerge. With increasing emphasis on the digitization of materials to provide full online access, academic libraries established institutional repositories to archive the historical and research output of their institutions, and digital repositories to manage digital images. Encoded Archival Description (EAD) allowed archives to put full descriptions and inventories of their collections online, though typically in yet another separate database. Add to this the growing number of aggregators providing online access to the full text of journal articles, and libraries were now faced with multiple databases containing library resources, with differing search interfaces and types and levels of metadata. The catalogue was no longer the central place to find all resources held or managed by the library, but primarily a finding device for physical materials that needed to be checked out or consulted in person in order to be used. In contrast, most other repositories provided full online access to the research content, which users could access without needing to be physically present in the library. In response, metasearch was born. The idea was to provide a single search interface across different databases and present results in a unified result set, so that users did not need to search each database separately. In practice, metasearch never achieved its initial promise, as variations in metadata standards and practice made unified search parameters difficult, and slow response time due to the query being sent to multiple databases made it a frustrating experience for users (Brown-Sica, Beall and McHale, 2010).

As the decade continued, the popularity of electronic books, or e-books, began to grow. Access to e-books was typically acquired in packages, similar to how electronic journal content is licensed, though often with additional restrictions regarding simultaneous use. Partly as a result of the impracticality of individual cataloguing by libraries of each title within an aggregated package, especially when individual titles could be added or rescinded at any time, publishers began providing Machine-Readable Cataloging (MARC) record sets with their packages. The quality of metadata in these MARC records varied greatly, but cataloguers developed skills in batch editing and loading of records, using applications such as MarcEdit (http://marcedit.reeset.net/) and OpenRefine (http://openrefine.org/). Individual libraries needed to weigh the costs and benefits of loading or not loading records for electronic content in their catalogues, depending on the availability of resources, system capabilities and staff skill sets (Traill, 2013).

The next and current phase of library catalogues is the discovery system, sometimes referred to as the discovery layer. A library discovery system differs from an OPAC in that it is completely separate and independent from the architecture of the back-end, staff side of the integrated library system. The goal of the discovery system is to integrate search and access from multiple sources including the library catalogue, but also full text of journal articles from licensed databases, and to provide options for indexing other repositories, such as finding aids and digital materials. While retaining Web 2.0 features including faceted browsing, the discovery system provides a better user experience than metasearch, as rather than send search queries simultaneously to the various databases, all metadata is indexed centrally. Vendors negotiate individually with content providers for access to full text, so coverage can vary, depending on which discovery platform the library chooses. Even with centrally indexed metadata, quality and standards are not always in synch, depending on the provider, so while search is improved and much more efficient, it is still not entirely reliable. Again, depending on which discovery layer the library employs, varying levels of local customization are possible for the user-interface.

What is a library resource?

To begin an in-depth exploration of what constitutes library resources, the collections grid developed by Lorcan Dempsey of OCLC Research provides a useful framework (Dempsey, 2009). The grid, adapted below in Figure 4.1, organizes resources according to the values of 'uniqueness' and 'stewardship/ scarcity'. The upper left quadrant of the grid contains those materials that have been traditionally viewed as library resources: tangible assets including books, journals, newspapers, government documents, DVDs, maps and scores. For these materials, we have well established workflows and standards for creating metadata and providing access in library catalogues, in the form of a surrogate descriptive record, if not full online access to the content. While these materials rank high on the stewardship scale, because we own and must physically manage them, they usually rank low in uniqueness. Many of these materials are widely held in libraries across the country or world, so a heavy investment in providing customized access to them can be called into question. Much of the work can be done for us through co-operative cataloguing, shelf-ready processing, the purchase of vendor records, and shared collection repositories.

		Stewardship	
		High	Low
Uniqueness	Low	Books and journals	Web resources
	High	Special collections	Research and learning materials

Figure 4.1 Collections grid

For licensed electronic resources, in many cases all that is needed is a link for local access; the metadata as well as the content do not need to be managed locally.

Moving to the upper right quadrant of the grid, we find those resources that rank low in both stewardship and uniqueness. This category includes freely accessible web resources, open source software, newsgroup archives and similar materials that are not created or managed by the local institution. While some of these materials may be of interest to library users, they are often not given high priority for integration into library catalogues. Because of the ephemeral nature of many of these resources, maintaining access over time can be labour intensive, and difficult to justify, given limited staff time.

The lower left quadrant of the grid includes those materials ranking high in both uniqueness and stewardship. These are primarily materials thought of as 'special collections', including archives, rare books, local history and manuscripts. This category can also include locally produced content such as theses and dissertations, whether in print or electronic form. While their value to the library and research community is rarely in question, for a long time the cataloguing of these materials was often neglected and inadequate, owing largely to their difficulty. Workflows were built around the bulk of standard, circulating materials, and unique and specialized materials were left for special projects, when extra staffing or funding was available. With the rise in shared metadata and shelf-ready processes, and increased attention in the last 15 to 20 years on 'hidden collections', effort at many libraries has been reallocated towards providing better access to these materials.

The lower right quadrant of the grid consists of those resources where interest and attention is now emerging in academic libraries. This includes research and learning materials such as research data, learning objects, courseware, online portfolios and other items where the library's stewardship role is less defined. Since these resources are highly unique and often institution-specific, the need for providing standardized, sustainable access to them is critical, but the method for doing this, and the building of relationships between librarians, researchers and content creators in order to make this happen in a consistent manner, is still in development.

The collections grid described in Figure 4.1 above was first presented in the mid-2000s, and since then many academic cataloguing departments have moved in the directions indicated. The availability of batch-level and shelf-ready processing of commercial and widely held resources has freed staff time to work more on rare and special materials. At one time considered to be distinct positions, the roles of cataloguers and metadata librarians have in many cases converged. Rather than confining themselves to item-level cataloguing of resources using traditional standards and formats such as the Anglo-American Cataloguing Rules (AACR), Resource Description and Access (RDA) and MARC, cataloguers are now working with multiple standards including Dublin Core, Metadata Encoding and Transmission Standard (METS) and Metadata Object Description Schema (MODS), providing consultation on access to digital resources, and working with institutional repositories and research data. At the same time, the economic recession has forced rethinking of priorities and library workflows, and in some cases the anticipated 'freed up' staff positions have been eliminated, or lost through attrition.

Granularity

Cataloguing standards generally provide guidelines for cataloguing materials at the level of the resource as a whole, as opposed to sub-sections of the resource. While on rare occasions a library might catalogue an individual book chapter or journal article, this is an exception to usual practice. As a result, titles and authors of individual journal articles were usually not searchable within the catalogue, nor were more specific subject terms that were relevant to the article but not captured by the broader subject headings applied to the record for the parent resource. In order to gain access to specific articles or chapters, researchers needed to consult indexing services and other reference materials, initially in print, but eventually in the form of online databases. In contrast, discovery platforms integrate metadata for library resources with article metadata to which the library has licensed access. The advantage of this is that it removes the need for a user to perform multiple searches. Many researchers are understandably unclear on what will appear in the catalogue and what will not, and at least in the case of journal articles, integrated discovery helps to alleviate that confusion. In addition, depending on the quality of the metadata for licensed resources, integrated discovery can allow for deeper and richer searches according to authors, subjects and keywords, which may not otherwise have appeared in the catalogue. A negative result of this integration is that the large number of article records (which include not only scholarly, peer-reviewed content, but reviews and newspaper articles) can easily flood search results, making it difficult for a researcher to pinpoint the precise thing they are looking for. Most discovery systems, however, allow for the customization of searches, by limiting them to library held resources, or selecting the types or formats of materials desired in the result set. Even if a broad, general search is initially performed, users can refine their searches or click on facets to lead them to more precise results.

Web-scale discovery systems have led to discussions of how to determine the appropriate level of granularity regarding search and access. In some disciplines, access to individual book chapters, or stanzas of poems, could be beneficial. For example, Alexander Street Press provides discipline-specific indexing at the item level for particular types of content in their databases. There are many factors to consider when providing access at various levels of specificity. Context is the key: it is important to know not only the identifying information for the segment of content that is being accessed, but also its relation to the larger whole. If individual series, files or items from a larger archival collection are catalogued, enough information must be provided to understand its provenance and the circumstances of its creation. Similarly, the minimal metadata often provided for images in digital repositories can sometimes be meaningless in a library catalogue without adequate contextual information and enhanced description. As is often the case when determining the appropriate level of access, desire for greater granularity must be weighed against availability of resources. Few libraries have enough staff to provide this type of granular access on a large scale. In addition, there are few, if any, widely recognized standards by which to create granular metadata, and most library cataloguing systems are unable to support it.

Multi-institutional repositories

In recent years, several multi-institutional repositories of digitized resources have been developed, providing libraries and library users with yet another source of access to a broad array of materials. Europeana (http://europeana.eu/portal) is a collaboration of cultural memory institutions across Europe, which includes content from hundreds of museums, national libraries and archives, and seeks to provide not only access but interconnection and cultural context. The Digital Public Library of America (DPLA; http://dp.la) is a similar project, featuring contributed digital images from repositories across the USA. The DPLA uses a model where smaller institutions, such as local historical societies, with limited resources can contribute their content via regional hubs, which normalize the metadata before submission to the central database. The HathiTrust (www. hathitrust.org) was established by academic libraries participating in the Google Books Project, as a shared repository of digitized books. In contrast to Europeana and DPLA, HathiTrust consists primarily of textual content. Full text access is available for all resources within the database that are in the public domain, while those still protected by copyright can be searched, and in some cases snippets are available to view.

These types of large-scale collaborations provide a treasure trove for researchers. In particular, the interfaces of Europeana and DPLA promote interactivity; they encourage users to create their own virtual sets, use application program interfaces to access and repackage the data in numerous ways, and link via social media. What place, if any, do these types of databases have within the context of a local discovery system?

For libraries that contributed digitized resources to these databases, a record might exist in the local catalogue that links to the digital version in the shared repository. While this added access can be advantageous to the users, and helps them retrieve useful resources, regardless of their starting point, interfaces should clearly indicate when the user is being taken outside the catalogue, and 'breadcrumbs' should be available to trace back to the starting point. Some libraries have also imported records for public domain titles within the HathiTrust into their local catalogues, whether or not the library has a print version of the resource. As with other types of freely available web content, the 'free' access needs to be weighed against the staff time and technology needed to complete the transaction and ensure that access is sustainable.

User-contributed data

As mentioned previously, with the advent of Web 2.0 catalogues, users were provided options to contribute their own data or content to library interfaces. Although in most cases these features have not been heavily used in library catalogues, the presence of user tags, reviews and annotations can also be considered library resources in a broad sense. When opening up catalogues to user-contributed data, libraries should establish and communicate policies regarding content, and have the option to remove inappropriate or inaccurate information. User-contributed data has been most successful in 'crowd-sourcing' projects, which request users to provide missing information regarding digital photographs, or to provide transcriptions of digitized print resources, such as diaries or theatre programmes. These projects are typically narrowly targeted and research-based, and not integrated into the catalogue's main interface. Crowd-sourcing of this type can provide data that can be used by library staff to enhance metadata records (Pecoskie, Spiteri and Tarulli, 2014).

Integration of library services

As previously mentioned, there was a time when OPACs were somewhat disconnected from the library web page. The front-end library home page would provide a link to the catalogue, which would take the user to a completely different service. With today's discovery layers and mobile-friendly interfaces, there is more seamless integration between the two. There is usually a search box prominently displayed at or near the top of the page, providing quick access to the catalogue. If the user wants more options than basic search, an advanced search option is a click away. Usability studies have shown that many library patrons make little or no distinction between the library home page and library catalogue, and a large percentage are going to the home page to search the catalogue (Larson and Hanson, 2015).

Additional library services, outside those typically considered part of the catalogue, can to varying degrees be integrated into the user workflow. Circulation, requests for holds on checked out items, interlibrary loans, scanning and reference or research help are all services that have traditionally been facilitated by library staff working at disparate service desks. Just as many libraries have now reduced their physical service points, combining formerly separate desks for reference, circulation, reserves and so forth, it is also possible in many cases to include library services within the catalogue, rather than require the user to visit other areas of the library home page, or even physical service points.

Fulfilment

If users locate a resource to which they would like access, the behind the scenes library processes that make their access possible need not be visible to the users. To illustrate this, consider a hypothetical academic library user who would like to learn about waterfowl migration. She performs a search in her library's catalogue, and finds a number of resources available in both print and electronic format. One of these resources is a recently published monograph on the subject. The catalogue indicates that this volume is available in the science library in print, and also as an e-book. If the user prefers print, she can click a button in the catalogue to request to have the book sent to her at her campus location. If the book she wants is checked out, she can request a recall or to be added to the waiting list for the book. If she prefers electronic format, the catalogue will check her credentials to see whether full access is available according to her user category. It is possible that the e-book is part of a Patron Driven or Demand Driven Acquisitions (PDA/DDA) program, where the library acquires access to the resource at the time a user expresses interest in it. This transaction should be seamless to the user: she need not know what acquisitions processes are invoked once she clicks through to consult the book. It is likely that the user is accessing the catalogue from home or her dormitory room via a mobile device. Depending on the library's user agreement, the user may be able to download the e-book to her tablet or smartphone.

The user's search also returned a number of relevant journal articles. Several of these were available in electronic journals to which the library has licensed access. From the catalogue interface, the user can print the articles, or save them to her online account to read later. She can also send citations to a citation manager program if she wishes to create a bibliography. Two of the articles are available in electronic journals, to which the library does not have access. The user should be presented with the option to request the articles through interlibrary loan. Once the transaction with the lending library is completed, the user will be e-mailed copies of the articles. Finally, one article is available only in print. The user can go to the shelf to retrieve the physical volume, or request that it be scanned and sent to her, if the library provides this service.

In summary, there are multitudes of ways in which libraries provide access to resources, but users should not need to jump through multiple hoops in order to have their needs fulfilled, depending on the source or format of the resource. The transactions should be as seamless as possible, with the user being presented with a clear set of menu options free of library jargon (e.g., 'request from another library', rather than 'interlibrary loan').

Customization

When users visit commercial websites, such as Amazon, they expect to receive customized service based on their user profile and their purchasing history. Similarly, services in a library catalogue can be customized to the background and interests of the user. In many library systems, including public and academic, library users have a personal account that stores their contact information and credentials, and grants them access to specific resources and services. For instance, a county public library may have co-operative borrowing agreements with libraries in surrounding communities regarding the checking out of print books, but only residents of the county may be allowed to check out or reserve e-books. In academic libraries, user accounts grant varying privileges to users based on their affiliation: undergraduates, graduate students, faculty, staff and unaffiliated users may all have different policies regarding for how long and how many materials can be checked out, whether overdue fines are applied, and the level of access to electronic resources. Library user accounts also typically include the ability to generate holds or requests for books checked out, and allow the user to save search queries and create virtual lists of materials of interest. Some catalogues may allow users to rate or comment on library resources, or tag records with keywords.

The services above are provided based on a very broad categorization of users: the catalogue verifies on login to what he or she has access, and which policies should be applied. But more personalized customization is possible. Recommender services, such as bX, a product of Ex Libris Group (Ex Libris, 2015), use aggregated data to suggest articles of interest based on the article the user is currently viewing. Other services might suggest resources based on previous search history. The University of Minnesota Libraries has used 'affinity strings' to recommend resources based on an anonymized user profile, such as graduate students in the College of Design (Hanson, Nackerud and Jensen, 2008).

When customized services are built at a local level, they allow for greater expansion of the definition of 'resources'. Along with lists of the major scholarly journals and reference books for the given subject, recommendations can also be provided for the most useful online indexes or databases to search, as well as special collections and archival materials available on campus related to the subject. In addition, users can be provided with the name and contact information of the library's subject liaison for their area of interest.

There are a variety of ways to push these types of personalized services to users. Links and menus on the library's home page can point users in the right direction. When a user logs in, they may see a link for 'recommendations', which will provide them with suggested resources as listed above. This still requires a bit of extra work on the users' part, however: they must know what to look for and be aware that they need extra help. Embedding customized and enhanced reference help within the search experience provides a more seamless workflow, and offers the users help at the time they need it, and sometimes even before they know they need it. The University of Michigan Library catalogue (www.lib.umich.edu) provides virtual reference help at the start of the search, and easy linking to services as the user navigates through the catalogue. Starting at the home page, the user is provided with a single search box. When a search term is entered, the user can choose the scope of the search by checking or unchecking boxes for various databases. Once the search is executed, the user is presented with a menu of resources in various categories. A search for the term 'Okinawa' returns a list of records for books from the catalogue, several online journal articles, and the names, photographs and contact information for four Asian studies librarians. At the top of the 'Research Help' listing is an 'Ask a Librarian' button, which opens up an instant messaging session. Depending on the subject, specific databases, online journals or library created web pages might be presented for further exploration. If the user clicks through to view one of the records from the catalogue, menu options at the bottom of the screen provide search tips and links to additional resources, such as course reserves and interlibrary loan. The 'Ask a Librarian' option also appears here.

While use of user profiles and search history can provide an improved and more seamless experience, it also raises issues of privacy. While users of the internet and, in particular, social networking sites such as Facebook are well aware that almost nothing they do online is private, the tracking and retention of data on library use by individuals is contrary to library values. When developing services that use patron data, libraries must be vigilant in striking a balance between improved service and privacy. Users should be made aware upfront if their demographic data or search history is being used, and be given the option to opt out. Other than transactional information, such as items requested or checked out, data should be used in an aggregated and anonymized fashion, and patron history should not be retained in a way that traces back to an individual once the transaction is complete.

Conclusion

While the broadened definition of library resources and the greater integration of disparate information sources and services into the catalogue is a benefit to users, it provides a number of challenges. Despite years of promotion and marketing of the many things a library provides, studies have shown that the majority of library users still have a very traditional view of what a library is. In a 2010 study by OCLC, for 75% of Americans, 'books' were still the first thing to come to mind when they think of libraries (Connaway, 2015; OCLC, 2010). The starting point for many users is not the library catalogue, but Google or other search engines. Even when licensed library resources are embedded in Google search results, such as Google Scholar, users are often unaware that they are actually accessing a library service, as the direct link to an online article would not be possible if their library did not pay for access.

In one sense, users do not need to know in all cases what the library is doing behind the scenes, as long as their research needs are being met. On the other hand, this can create the false impression that 'everything is online', and that libraries, seen only as a warehouse for print materials or perhaps a quiet study space, are less essential. Libraries have tried various methods for branding their services and making their user base aware of the services they provide, but with users' limited attention spans, it is not always clear that this message is getting across.

A major ongoing challenge is the cost of technology, which includes not only hardware and software, but the human resources needed for configuration, programming, metadata creation and maintenance. Cloud services can save institutions the cost of maintaining server space, but necessitate a trade-off over customization and local control.

Another challenge is the consistency and quality of metadata. Long gone are the days when cataloguers believed that everything, no matter what the format, should be in a MARC record maintained (and often customized) in the local catalogue. With the disparate types and formats of materials now represented in the catalogue, which come from multiple sources, such a model is no longer realistic or sustainable, if it ever was. In future libraries should embrace concepts of linked data and the Semantic Web (see chapter 3). Metadata from different sources and schemas can intermingle with careful attention to relationships between different types of data, and standards for how to combine or use them within the information framework. No database is every going to be clean or perfect, but tools exist that can manipulate batches of data at a broad scale, and identify inconsistency and anomalies.

Sweeping technological and societal change has led to a broadening of the definition of library resources, and to the services libraries provide, as well as the methods for offering those services. Users expect to interact electronically, and often remotely, without apparent human intervention, from wherever they happen to be, and with whatever electronic device is most convenient to them. In many ways, libraries are meeting the challenges these changes have caused, but we must continue to find new ways to serve the information needs of our users. The library metadata community is at the threshold of broad and sweeping change, but with enough energy to move forward, we have the promise of fuller integration with the broader information universe on the horizon.

References

Brown-Sica, M., Beall, J. and McHale, N. (2010) Next Generation Library Catalogs and the Problem of Slow Response Time, *Information Technology and Libraries*, **29**, 214–23.

Connaway, L. S. (2015) *The Library in the Life of the User: engaging with people where they live and learn*, OCLC Research, www.oclc.org/content/dam/research/publications/2015/oclcresearch-library-in-life-of-user.pdf.

Dempsey, L. (2009) Web-sightings, weblog, 11 March, http://orweblog.oclc.org/archives/001897.html.

Ex Libris (2015) bX Usage-Based Services Transform Your Discovery Experience!, http://www.exlibrisgroup.com/category/bXUsageBasedServices.

Hanson, C., Nackerud, S. and Jensen, K. (2008) Affinity Strings: enterprise data for resource recommendations, *Code4Lib Journal*, December, http://purl.umn.edu/46576.

Larson, E. and Hanson, C. (2015) Put Your Money Where the Mouse Is: tools and techniques for making informed design decisions, http://hdl.handle.net/11299/170655.

OCLC (2010) *Perceptions of Research,* Online Computer Library Center, www.oclc.org/content/dam/oclc/reports/2010perceptions/ 2010perceptions_all_singlepage.pdf.

Pecoskie, J., Spiteri, L. and Tarulli, L. (2014) OPACs, Users, and Readers' Advisory: exploring the implications of user-generated content for readers' advisory in Canadian public libraries, *Cataloging & Classification Quarterly,* **52**, 431–53.

Smith-Yoshimura, K. (2012) *Social Metadata for Libraries, Archives, and Museums: executive summary,* OCLC Research, www.oclc.org/research/publications/library/2012/2012-01r.html.

Traill, S. (2013) Quality Issues in Vendor-Provided e-Monograph Records, *Library Resources & Technical Services,* **57** (4), 213–26.

Note

1   www.lib.ncsu.edu/endeca/presentations.html.

CHAPTER 5

Managing volume in discovery systems

Aaron Tay

The well established measures of recall and precision are becoming increasingly relevant in web-scale discovery systems. Given the way that most people search, which is by using the simple keyword box that searches all text anywhere in the record, web-scale discovery systems will lead to increasingly large recall as we provide access to more linked items. Using the environment of academic libraries, this chapter will explore the following questions: Do we need to be careful about the sheer volume of items to which we can provide access via web-scale discovery systems? Do we want these systems to become another Google, where precision of results is not always as accurate as we would like? Are we too obsessed with the notion of providing access to everything at the expense of the quality of the results?

Introduction – the promise of the one search

'The Library with a Thousand Databases' was the amazingly

evocative title of a talk given by Matthew Reidsma as part of NISO's Virtual Conference on Web-Scale Discovery in 2013 (Reidsma, 2013). Drawing on Joseph Campbell's work on myth, *The Hero with a Thousand Faces* (Campbell, 1968), Reidsma drew a parallel between Campbell's 'hero's journey', where the aspiring hero ventures from the normal world (use of Google) to the special realm (use of specialized databases), and the experiences first time users face as they start a piece of academic research. A similar idea can be seen in the series of videos *The Adventures of Sir Learnsalot*, where academic research is depicted as a hero's journey (Tolly, 2013). The use of a library web-scale discovery system, Summon, was then proposed by Reidsma as a partial solution to keep users in the 'normal world', at least as much as possible. This is an interesting analogy, though I would argue that the challenge a first time user faces when starting an academic research project goes beyond just using databases, but there is no doubt that web-scale discovery does make things easier from the point of view of searching.

Web-scale discovery systems like Summon[1] and its competitors are generally designed to be easy to use and try to mimic web search engines in terms of usability. This was unlike online public accesses systems, which forced users to search in unnatural ways by inverting the author name, and which had generally unappealing user interfaces that were designed more for expert users. While the usability of 'next generation catalogues' that preceded them improved greatly by including features such as a one search box with relevancy ranking, facets and 'did you mean' features, they still did not resonate with users, because they only searched for books and DVDs from the local catalogue, and lacked the ability to search for articles in subscribed databases in one search. Arguably the strongest feature that web-scale discovery brings beyond enhanced usability is the promise to search through multiple silos of content in databases in one uniform search interface.

Unlike the older generation of federated search systems, which had problems with speed and reliability (Helfer and Wakimoto, 2005), web-scale discovery systems can sidestep this issue. By acquiring the content from content providers in advance, harmonizing the data, and putting this data into one central unified single index for searching, web-scale discovery accomplishes the task of a 'single search' at the cost of a slight time lag in the currency of results. Unlike federated search, web-scale discovery search results are not retrieved in real time from the databases, which can lead to results that can be several days, if not weeks, old. For example, newspaper results retrieved from web-scale discovery systems could be a few days older than from a federated search, but many would consider this a fair trade-off in return for a search that is more stable and has a faster response time.

While there was initial debate over whether centralized index searching alone was sufficient, or whether one should create a hybrid approach of centralized index and federated searching (Katzman, 2009), today most academic libraries have shifted towards using one of the four major web-scale discovery systems: Summon, Primo, EBSCO Discovery Service (EDS) and WorldCat Discovery,[2] which are all based primarily, if not solely, on central index (Breeding, 2015).

Of course, for users accustomed to Google, the idea that you need painstakingly to rerun the same search in different databases to search for what you want is absurd; how web-scale discovery works is the normal expected state of affairs. Librarians acknowledge this, and in a 2012 survey of Association of Research

Libraries institutions that used Summon, many chose to brand their search as 'one search' or variants such as 'searchall' (Tay, 2012). The concept of one search is very seductive and obvious to users, and the idea that one should stuff as much as possible into one search seems to be uncontroversial; yet, as we shall see, trying to put in as much content as possible into a web-scale discovery search index has led to many problems, and most libraries choose instead to curate the content that is searchable in their web-scale discovery.

The rush to 'everything'

In the early days of web-scale discovery systems, one of their selling points was the amount of content included in the index. One of the most important considerations for librarians when selecting web-scale discovery is whether it included databases to which their institution subscribes (Hoeppner, 2012). In their early days, web-scale discovery systems owned by ProQuest, EBSCO and others were announcing content agreements with content providers almost monthly, and as time went by, content providers such as Elsevier, Sage and Taylor & Francis started to provide their content to these systems, to avoid risking reduced visibility, as results showed increased usage of content included in web-scale discovery indexes (Way, 2010).

While it made sense for full text publishers to contribute content to discovery services, the value proposition for abstracting and indexing databases to contribute their metadata was not as clear. As noted in the National Information Standards Organization (NISO) Open Discovery Initiative (ODI) survey report on libraries and content providers conducted in 2012, 'the majority of these respondents reported perceived risk to the value-added data available in their abstracting/indexing (A&I) databases and the need for identification of supplied content in the databases. Some content provider comments touched on tensions where the evolution of discovery services is seen by some as an alternative to traditional A&I services' (NISO ODI Working Group, 2013, 10). It is difficult, if not impossible, to quantify the value of contributing metadata from abstracting and indexing databases to discovery services. Web-scale discovery systems that merged metadata from various contributing sources, including full text publishers, aggregators and abstracting and indexing databases, would often increase the retrieval of full text resources, but at the expense of hiding the contribution made by the value-added metadata contributed by the abstracting and indexing source. For example, an item could be found solely due to a match in the value-added metadata contributed by the abstracting and indexing source to the discovery service, however on clicking on the result, the user would be directed immediately to a full text source on another platform. This would be recorded as a full text download on the other platform, but usage of the abstracting and indexing source might actually plunge, as the user never actually visits the abstracting and indexing source. That being said, as of today, two of the largest generalist abstracting and indexing databases, Web of Science and Scopus, are generally available in discovery services.

One of the greatest contentions was the role played by two web-scale discovery systems, Summon, and EDS. Unlike the other two discovery services, WorldCat Discovery Service and Primo, they were both owned by aggregators of content (ProQuest and EBSCO respectively), and played a role as a discovery service provider. The concerns were twofold. First was the fear that these discovery services would privilege their own content in the relevancy ranking, as compared with more 'content neutral' services. Second is the fact that unlike publishers such as Sage or Taylor & Francis, which were generally happy to provide their content (both full text and metadata) to all four major discovery services, there was concern that ProQuest and EBSCO would not provide their own content to other discovery services. A well known dispute occurred among the Orbis Cascade Alliance, Ex Libris and EBSCO about releasing metadata from some EBSCO databases subscribed to by the Alliance, to be displayed in Ex Libris' Primo (see series of letters in Orbis Cascade Alliance, 2013). This led librarians like Carl Grant to warn about libraries 'being locked into a content silo', depending on the type of discovery service they selected (Grant, 2013). This issue has recently eased to some extent with ProQuest signing deals with Ex Libris (Proquest, 2014) and EBSCO releasing a policy of sharing metadata (Quint, 2014), though problems still remain. Today, a typical academic library can provide access to a substantial majority of its subscribed content in a typical discovery service, with the actual amount depending on the fit between the subscribed content and the discovery service chosen.

The rush to content has created a mindset where some librarians would add and squeeze everything possible into the index for searching and let the relevancy ranking sort out the results. This 'everything' includes:

- subscribed content from publishers and aggregators
- subscribed content from abstracting and indexing services
- local content from the library including, catalogues, and institutional and digital repositories, LibGuides, etc.
- free and open access content.

Putting as much of their content as possible into one discovery index achieves what Lorcan Dempsey calls 'full collection discovery', where one can search for all or most of the library's collection in one search box (Dempsey, 2012). Other libraries have gone even further to achieve what is known as 'full library discovery', by including content such as library web pages and FAQs, and even highlighting librarians and expertise in search results (Dempsey, 2012).

Google Scholar, the largest academic material index?

How large should our library discovery index aspire to be? A natural idea would be to try to benchmark against Google Scholar, which is a major commercial competitor to our library discovery services. Various reports suggest that many of our users, including faculty and postgraduates, are increasingly turning towards Google Scholar for discovery purposes (Bosman and Kramer, 2015; JISC, 2012). It might therefore be instructive to consider the size of the Google Scholar index as a standard against which to compare our library discovery index.

Although Google Scholar is often seen as the largest index of academic material, its exact size has not been disclosed by Google, which has not stopped many from trying to quantify it. The size of Google Scholar was estimated to be 100 million records, as of May 2014 (Khabsa and Giles, 2014). Using a range of methods, Orduña-Malea et al. (2014) estimated the size of Google Scholar to be between 126.3 million and 176.8 million records.

How large are web-scale discovery systems in comparison with Google Scholar? The only data I can find is for Summon, though the other three discovery services should be in the same range. In

2014, Summon contained 2.1 billion de-duped records but, more importantly, approximately 142.8 million items in the index are 'from commercial and open access resources that are available for clients to access based on their individual subscriptions' (Proquest, 2015). This 142.8 million total is roughly comparable to the size of the estimated Google Scholar index found by the stated studies. For someone new to web-scale discovery, this seems to be good news, as our web-scale discovery indexes seem to be the same size as our commercial rival, and to be competitive we should try to make searchable everything possible in the index, including:

- items in the library local catalogue or institutional repository
- articles in the index to which the library subscribes
- open access articles in the index
- items to which the library does not subscribe.

A naive approach would be to adopt a 'put them all in the index and let the relevancy ranking sort it out' approach, and make it all searchable. Yet in practice few libraries make the third and fourth items listed above searchable, and some libraries even refuse to create a blended search of catalogue items and subscribed articles, and separate the search results from the first two items above in different search boxes, because a single blended list can bury relevant results.

The collection spectrum in discovery

Libraries today have more fluid boundaries on what counts as their collection; for example the library collection can include:

- purchased and physically stored collections
- licensed online collections
- demand driven acquisition collections (print or online)
- shared print collections (available via consortium agreements)
- open access and free online collections.

Dempsey, Malpas and Lavoie, 2014

Which of the above sets of information should be shown when searching? While some libraries include content to which they have no access (MIT Libraries for instance), most do not. Part of the reason is because a large target of such services is undergraduates, who expect their library discovery service to show only items to which they have immediate access. Faculty members who have outsourced their discovery needs elsewhere, such as to Google, Google Scholar and Google Books, and use discovery services only to check if an item is available, also expect discovery services to list only what is immediately available, so most libraries choose not to show items that are not available.

What about open access and free items? While making all available open access resources searchable seems to be a good idea, we find that in practice many libraries steer away from adding available open access collections. There are many reasons for this, such as the poor quality of some of these collections, many broken links, and links to non-free full text resources (Renaville, 2015). Finally, many academic libraries are beginning to argue against the obvious 'blended' approach of including in one result list items normally found in a catalogue, together with articles from bibliographic databases. Some argue that a blended model that mixes different classes of content in one list confuses less experienced users, who are unaware of the differences between book and article results (Rochkind, 2012; Tay and Yikang, 2015). Notably, even Google Scholar generally shows only articles, and rarely shows books. This has led to the rise of the idea that a 'bento style' approach might be better, separating the display of results from different silos in different containers on the same page, rather than showing only one blended list of results. Libraries at universities such as North Carolina State, Duke and Stanford now employ this type of search (Lown, Sierra and Boyer, 2013).

Why relevancy ranking with everything is hard

Librarians have found that an approach that throws everything into the index and lets the relevancy ranking sort it out does not work. The weakness in relevancy ranking has manifested itself in two ways:

- known item search, where the wanted item does not appear on the first page
- topic search, where the precision of the results is often very poor.

As noted by various experts like Marshall Breeding and Roger Schonfeld, one of the major problems with web-scale discovery is known item search (Breeding, 2015; Schonfeld, 2014). In addition to anecdotal stories from librarians who have implemented web-scale discovery, some studies have found serious problems with known item searching in web-scale discovery systems. In a random sample test of known items queries using Summon, Namei and Young (2015) found that only 70% of queries succeeded in ranking relevant items in the top ten results. As known item searches make up an estimated 44% to 50% of search queries in a typical library discovery system, (Chapman et al., 2013; Schlembach, Mischo and Bishoff, 2013), a 30% failure rate in what is considered a simple basic task is extremely serious. Similarly, Singley (2014) found that testing with single word titles, titles with stop words, title or author keyword, and citations led to failures for many library discovery services, ranging from only 20% to slightly over 90% success rates. While some of the problems, such as searching with complete citations, have since been remedied, not all problems have been solved.

Why have library systems regressed to the point where simple known item searching has become difficult? While it is true such systems do not browse titles, a keyword search is generally sufficient for known item searches in next generation catalogues that include only local items.

Obviously, it is the greater mass of possible matches due to the inclusion of millions of articles in the unified index that makes matching not so clear cut, particularly for local material from the catalogue, such as hard copy books, microforms and so forth. This is also one reason why the bento search approaches mentioned above have become popular. Always showing the first five or ten results of every category of items sidesteps this problem, although other approaches, such as using search assistance to detect known item searches and recommend links, might help. Such an approach is employed by the University of Illinois Urbana-Champaign Library (Mischo, Schlembach and Norman, 2013).

What impacts discoverability?

It is not just known item searching that suffers in web-scale discovery systems, but also subject searching. Web-scale discovery systems struggle with relevancy ranking because of the diversity of content types (in length and type of metadata) they need to rank. Unlike Google Scholar, or almost any type of library database, which ranks the relevancy of only one type of material, web-scale discovery systems attempt to rank the relevancy of a variety of items, including books, book chapters, articles, DVDs, online videos, microforms, music CDs, and more. This is very problematic, because each type of material differs greatly in whether the full text is available for indexing, as well as the amount of metadata available.

As web-scale discovery systems can only work with the metadata or full text they are provided by content providers, they get content that ranges from the most minimal metadata, for example, e-book records with only title, author and a broad subject, to fully described 'thick metadata', including fully described controlled subject headings, tables of contents, and reviews found in abstract and indexing databases. Full text may or may not be available for indexing either, depending on the content provider, or the type of content indexed; for example, discovery services may include many non-text material, such as streaming videos, and print books with no full text available from electronic copies. Clearly, relevancy ranking becomes extremely difficult because of the diversity and range of full text and metadata available. Figure 5.1 shows one possible way to visualize the diversity of content with which the relevancy ranking must work.

On the horizontal axis, we have content that ranges from having full text to those without full text. On the vertical axis, we have content that ranges from having full metadata to those with thin metadata. Some examples of the type of content in the four quadrants include:

A thick metadata, no full text – e.g., abstracting and indexing databases, such as Scopus, Web of Science, APA Psycinfo

B thick metadata, full text – e.g., EBSCO databases in the EDS, combined super-records in Summon that include metadata from abstracting and indexing databases such as Scopus, and full text from publishers

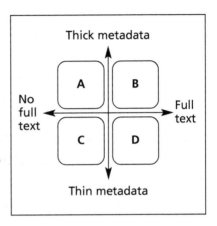

Figure 5.1
Two dimensions of content discovery

C thin metadata, no full text – e.g., publisher provided metadata with no full text, online video collections and institutional repository records

D thin metadata, full text – e.g., many publishers provide content to Summon or Primo, and so forth.

Obviously items in quadrant C with minimal metadata and no full text are often difficult to discover if the web-scale discovery service matches on both metadata and full text.

The problems with low precision and high recall

We can now understand why it can be difficult for known item searches for certain items (e.g., catalogue items with short generic titles) to produce relevant results. A web-scale discovery service that matches on both full text and metadata will have extremely high recall, as with Google or Google Scholar, but at the expense of precision, which can often be fatal for known item searches, which have an expectation of high precision. In such searches, users expect their results to appear near the top of the page or, at most, on the first page (typically ten results per page). In such a situation, overall recall is almost irrelevant, as the expectation of the searcher is that recall for a known item will be 100%, assuming the item exists. A result that ranks the desired item in the 100th position, while still achieving 100% recall, for example, would be useless. Unless carefully managed, the results of known item searches of local catalogue items with minimal metadata will often be buried, particularly if the title is short and generic. Non-text items such as music CDs, microforms or even books with no full text indexed suffer, particularly if they have short common titles. Known item searches are not the only type of search that suffers from low precision; subject searches can easily be affected for the same reason.

As the most relevant items might not have the most complete metadata or even full text, it is not necessarily the case that they will be ranked highly. While the relevancy ranking can be fine-tuned to a point, in general, the larger the index searched, the greater the recall, but at the price of precision; beyond a certain point, it can get problematic. Once again, it is perhaps instructive to review Google Scholar and the experience medical librarians had with using Google Scholar for systematic reviews. In a study of the use of Google Scholar for systematic reviews, Gehanno, Rolling and Darmoni (2013) concluded that 100% of the 738 studies retrieved for systematic reviews could be found in Google Scholar, leading to hopes that one could just use Google Scholar to find such studies and forgo the tedious need to set up search strategies for multiple databases. Unfortunately, hopes were dashed when it was found that while Google Scholar theoretically had extremely high recalls, the precision of searches was so low that it was not practical to use it for systematic reviews. The study estimated that because of the much lower precision of the results, users had to 'check about 20 times more references on relevance compared with the standard approach using multiple searches in traditional literature databases' (Boeker, Vach and Motschall, 2013).

Boeker, Vach, and Motschall (2013) suggested that Google Scholar queries had inherently low precision compared with databases, because of the lack of advanced search features. For instance, Google Scholar lacks deep nesting and truncation operations, and has a 256 character search limit, which limits the ability to create complicated precise searches. This, together with the auto-stemming capabilities of Google Scholar, results in searches with extremely low precision. While most library web-scale discovery services such as Summon, Primo or EDS support some of the missing features in Google Scholar, such as truncation, they are also generally not used for systematic reviews alone because of low precision caused by the large size of the index and matching of full text.

Practical advice for handling content in web-scale discovery services

Think carefully about the type of users you have, and the role your web-scale discovery service should play in the repertoire of search tools available to your users. Should the discovery service strive to be the broadest possible search tool, when tools like Google Scholar already play this role? Or should it aim for the sweet spot of being broader than individual library databases, yet better curated and more targeted than Google Scholar?

What type of searchable content should you add to the index? If your discovery service allows you to display items not owned or licensed by your institution, should you set that to be default? The answer to that question would depend on the sophistication of your users. If, as is the case in most academic libraries, you decide on a more restrained approach of only including items owned or licensed by your institution, should you add every available free or open access collection possible into the index for searching? Adding content to be searchable in your discovery service just because you can, and 'just in case', is often a bad idea, particularly in areas or subjects you know your users are unlikely to want to use, as precision is likely to suffer. Adding the PubMed Central collection, for example, or free foreign-language collections when your users do not generally look for such materials might be a bad idea, because while these additions might improve recall slightly, the precision of the results will be more adversely affected. Even subscribed content that presumably matches the type of content that users might want to see might not be an automatic inclusion. For example, you may consider not adding newspaper collections from providers like Factiva, even if the items are discoverable in the index. This is because newspaper collections tend to have faulty links, in addition to the sheer mass of newspaper articles that can often bury other results.

Be familiar with the options your discovery service offers. If your discovery service provides the option of metadata only search, but excludes full text as a default, you may want to test with a series of actual known item searches as well as typical topical search to see if the relevancy of results improves using metadata only but no full text search, or whether you can get away with including full text search. Also, check if your discovery service provides the option of adjusting the relevancy ranking: some systems might allow you to increase the weight of local holdings broadly, which may help with known item search of such items, and help prevent them from being buried by the articles in the index, while others may allow more specific changing of field weights. Above all, test with actual popular queries made by users, with an extra focus on items that have no full text and poor metadata. Depending on your source of data, e-books or other material might have very poor metadata as well. Investigate if your discovery system provides or allows the possibility of a recommender system for search assistance that can be customized, as this can help with searches that have poor relevancy.

Conclusion and the future of web-scale discovery

While implementing and maintaining web-scale discovery has become an expected part of academic librarianship, there is a brewing debate over whether libraries should continue to fight for a central role in discovery, or to cede to commercial and other services that operate at the network layer such as Google, Google Scholar or Mendeley. Utrecht University, for example, announced its decision to focus on delivery, and surrendered discovery to Google Scholar, Google and WorldCat (Kortekaas, 2012). This university has reason to believe that discovery happens elsewhere, as evidence suggests that the library website is not the starting place for discovery, not only for undergraduates (Perruso, 2015), but also for researchers (Housewright, Schonfeld and Wulfson, 2013). As the popularity of tools like Google Scholar as a general search system continues to skyrocket, is the best move for academic libraries to bow out of the discovery business? If that is the case, Utrecht University asks, why fight the change? One should, instead, focus on supporting delivery wherever the user is, whether via the Google Scholar library links program, OCLC or other service providers. More recently, Utrecht University designed a Chrome extension that would alert off-campus users whether any domains they are using can be proxied for nearly seamless access. The ultimate aim would be to focus on supporting researchers to use Google Scholar and library subject databases, and to do away with discovery services or even catalogues (Utrecht University, 2015). A similar idea would be to focus on supporting mainly known item search only in library systems and leave discovery to other systems.

Not everyone agrees with such a view, of course. Ken Varnum believes that individual institutions can have an edge over global systems like Google Scholar by creating specially tuned discovery services that include features, in particular scopes, which appeal specifically to their unique communities and cannot be easily duplicated by Google Scholar. The University of Michigan Library, for example, built an experimental tool that created collections of journals based on subject librarians' categorization of journal titles by subject and by one of three categories: novice, expert or both. Novice journal titles have articles that were more accessible and popular, while expert journal titles have articles that are more narrowly focused and specialized (Varnum, 2014).

An even more granular approach would be for librarians to scope collections around various controlled and uncontrolled subject terms. When the user logs into the tool the system would be able to identify the course in which the user is enrolled, and offer an option to only search within resources identified by the librarian to be suitable for this course. So, for example when a student enrolled in a basic Economics 101 course searches for 'depression', he or she could get results from journals identified by the Economics subject librarian suitable for that level of study.

Faced with competition from Google, Google Scholar, Mendeley and other non-library discovery services, academic libraries are at a crossroad. In one future path, academic libraries could decide that it was inevitable that they will lose their central position as a discovery source, and thus choose to maintain a minimum level of investments in library discovery services in preparation for obsolescence. Such an approach is not without risks, as the long term sustainability of commercial tools like Google Scholar cannot be taken for granted. Also, as mentioned previously, as good as tools like Google Scholar are for exploratory searches, they still lack the precision we get from focused subject databases. In another future path, academic libraries could decide to focus on differentiating their discovery tools from commercial services, by creating custom features that are the best fit for their individual communities, as suggested by Varnum (2014). Perhaps by combining librarians' subject expertise and knowledge of the community with search and ranking algorithms, a more precise yet broad tool can be created.

References

Boeker, M., Vach, W. and Motschall, E. (2013) Google Scholar as Replacement for Systematic Literature Searches: good relative recall and precision are not enough, *BMC Medical Research Methodology*, **13** (1), 131.

Bosman, J. and Kramer, B. (2015) *First 1000 Responses – most popular tools per research activity*, 23 June, https://101innovations.wordpress.com/2015/06/23/first-1000-responses-most-popular-tools-per-research-activity.

Breeding, M. (2015) *The Future of Library Resource Discovery*, white paper, National Information Standards Organization.

Campbell, J. (1968) *The Hero with a Thousand Faces*, 2nd edn, Princeton University Press.

Chapman, S., Desai, S., Hagedorn, K., Varnum, K., Mishra, S. and Piacentine, J. (2013) Manually Classifying User Search Queries on an Academic Library Web Site, *Journal of Web Librarianship*, **7** (4), 401–21.

Dempsey, L. (2012) Thirteen Ways of Looking at Libraries, Discovery, and the Catalog: scale, workflow, attention, *Educause Review Online*, **88**, http://er.educause.edu/articles/2012/12/thirteen-ways-of-looking-at-libraries-discovery-and-the-catalog-scale-workflow-attention.

Dempsey, L., Malpas, C.and Lavoie, B. (2014) Collection Directions: the evolution of library collections and collecting, *Libraries and the Academy*, **14** (3), 392–423.

Gehanno, J.-F., Rollin, L. and Darmoni, S. (2013) Is the Coverage of Google Scholar Enough to be Used Alone for Systematic Reviews?, *BMC Medical Informatics and Decision Making*, **13** (1), 7.

Grant, C. (2013) *Do-They-Or-Don't-They? Ex Libris & EBSCO Information Services: content-neutrality & content silos; a living example of why librarians should pay attention when warned of the dangers of content silos*, 13 June, http://thoughts.care-affiliates.com/2013/06/do-they-or-dont-they-ex-libris-ebsco_13.html.

Helfer, D. and Wakimoto, J. C. (2005) Metasearching: the good, the bad, and the ugly of making it work in your library, *Searcher*, **13** (2), 40.

Hoeppner, A. (2012) The Ins and Outs of Evaluating Web-Scale Discovery Services, *Computers in Libraries*, **32** (3), 6.

Housewright, R., Schonfeld, R. C. and Wulfson, K. (2013) *Ithaka S+R US Faculty Survey 2012*, www.sr.ithaka.org/wp-content/mig/reports/Ithaka_SR_US_Faculty_Survey_2012_FINAL.pdf.

JISC (2012) *Researchers of Tomorrow: the research behaviour of Generation Y doctoral students*, Joint Information Systems Committee, www.webarchive.org.uk/wayback/archive/20140614040703/http://www.jisc.ac.uk/publications/reports/2012/researchers-of-tomorrow.aspx.

Katzman, D. (2009) *Is Speed Worth It? Federated search vs. unified index*, 30 October, http://deepwebtechblog.com/is-speed-worth-it-federated-search-vs-unified-index.

Khabsa, M. and Giles, C. L. (2014) *The Number of Scholarly Documents on the Public Web*, http://journals.plos.org/plosone/article?id= 10.1371/journal.pone.0093949.

Kortekaas, S. (2012) *Thinking the Unthinkable: a library without a catalogue; reconsidering the future of discovery tools for Utrecht University*, 4 September, http://libereurope.eu/blog/2012/09/04/ thinking-the-unthinkable-a-library-without-a-catalogue-reconsidering-the-future-of-discovery-tools-for-utrecht-university-library/.

Lown, C., Sierra, T. and Boyer, J. (2013) How Users Search the Library from a Single Search Box, *College & Research Libraries*, **74** (3), 227–41.

Mischo, W. H., Schlembach, M. C. and Norman, M. A. (2013) Modeling Search Assistance Mechanisms Within Web-Scale Discovery Systems. In *JDCL'13: proceedings of the 13th ACM/IEEE-CS joint conference on Digital libraries*, Association for Computing Machinery.

Namei, E. and Young, C. A. (2015) Measuring Our Relevancy: comparing results in a web-scale discovery tool, Google & Google Scholar, www.ala.org/acrl/sites/ala.org.acrl/files/content/ conferences/confsandpreconfs/2015/Namei_Young.pdf.

NISO ODI Working Group (2013) *ODI Survey Report: reflections and perspectives on discovery services; promoting transparency in discovery*, National Information Standards Organization, www.niso.org/ apps/group_public/document.php?document_id=9977.

Orbis Cascade Alliance (2013) *Ebsco and Exlibris*, www.orbiscascade.org/ebsco-ex-libris.

Orduña-Malea, E., Ayllón, J. M., Martín-Martín, A. and López-Cózar, E. D. (2014) About the Size of Google Scholar: playing the numbers, *Scientometrics*, **104** (3), 931–49.

Perruso, C. (2015) *Undergraduates' Use of Google vs. Library Resources: a four-year cohort study*,
http://crl.acrl.org/content/early/2015/11/05/crl15-826.full.pdf.

Proquest (2014) *ProQuest Collections Are Now Indexed and Discoverable through the Central Index of Ex Libris Primo*, www.proquest.com/about/news/2014/ProQuest-Collections-Are-Now-Indexed-and-Discoverable-through-the-Central-Index-of-Ex-Libris-Primo.html.

Proquest (2015) *Summon Index Growth: a review of 2014*, 2 February, www.proquest.com/blog/pqblog/2015/WFS2015-Summon-Index-Growth.html.

Quint, B. (2014) *EBSCO Opens Masses of Content to Third-Party Discovery Services*, 6 May,
http://newsbreaks.infotoday.com/NewsBreaks/EBSCO-Opens-Masses-of-Content-to-ThirdParty-Discovery-Services-96783.asp.

Reidsma, M. (2013) *The Library with a Thousand Databases*,
26 November, http://matthew.reidsrow.com/articles/58.

Renaville, F. (2015) *Open Access and Discovery Tools: how do Primo libraries manage green open access collections?*,
http://arxiv.org/abs/1509.04524.

Rochkind, J. (2012) *Article Search Improvement Strategy*, 2 October,
https://bibwild.wordpress.com/2012/10/02/article-search-improvement-strategy/.

Schlembach, M. C., Mischo, W. H. and Bishoff, J. (2013) The Use of Transaction Logs to Model User Searching Behaviours, *Qualitative and Quantitative Methods in Libraries*, **4**, 365–69.

Schonfeld, R. C. (2014) *Does Discovery Still Happen in the Library?*,
24 September, www.sr.ithaka.org/blog/does-discovery-still-happen-in-the-library-roles-and-strategies-for-a-shifting-reality/.

Singley, E. (2014) *Discovery Systems – testing known item searching*,
8 March, http://emilysingley.net/discovery-systems-testing-known-item-searching.

Tay, A. (2012) *Branding Library Discovery Services – what are libraries doing?*, 17 June, http://musingsaboutlibrarianship.blogspot.sg/2012/06/branding-library-discovery-services.html.

Tay, A. and Yikang, F. (2015) Implementing a Bento-Style Search in LibGuides v2, *Code4Lib Journal*, **29**, http://journal.code4lib.org/articles/10709.

Tolly, L. (2013) The Information Quest: mapping the information adventure to 'The Hero's Journey' of Joseph Campbell's Monomyth. In Walsh, A. and Coonan, E. (eds), *Only Connect ... discovery pathways, library explorations, and the information adventure*, Lulu.

Utrecht University (2015) *UU Easy Access – browser extension*, www.uu.nl/en/university-library/about-the-library/uu-easy-access-browser-extension-beta.

Varnum, K. (2014) Library Discovery: from ponds to streams. In Varnum, K. J. (ed.), *The Top Technologies Every Librarian Needs to Know: a LITA guide*, ALA TechSource.

Way, D. (2010) The Impact of Web-Scale Discovery on the Use of a Library Collection, *Serials Review*, **36** (4), 214–20.

Notes

1   www.proquest.com/products-services/The-Summon-Service.html.
2   See www.proquest.com/products-services/The-Summon-Service.html, www.exlibrisgroup.com/category/PrimoOverview, www.ebscohost.com/discovery and www.oclc.org/worldcat-discovery.en.html.

CHAPTER 6
Managing outsourced metadata in discovery systems

Laurel Tarulli

Introduction

A librarian sits at his or her work station, assisting students with questions about what to read next, checking in book returns and, when a quiet moment presents itself, cataloguing the new books and entering them into the library catalogue. With a simple title search within the catalogue, the vendor's discovery system identifies whether or not the book is a new title. If the title is new, a selection of Machine-Readable Cataloging (MARC) records is presented. The records are often pulled from libraries sharing the same vendor discovery system or consortium, or from the vendor itself. The librarian chooses a record, edits it as needed, and adds the book to the growing collection available for discovery in the library's catalogue. With ease and efficiency, the librarian is able to add titles to the collection, while continuing day-to-day tasks within the library.

This is a common, everyday practice among thousands, if not tens of thousands of librarians each day. It happens in school, public, special and academic libraries. The availability of records for downloading or sharing from consortia and, increasingly, vendors assists librarians, and greatly reduces the need for time-intensive original cataloguing and, in many cases, the editing of simple, bare-bones MARC records. The benefit of these records for download, sharing, or editing should not be disputed. Indeed, this chapter will take the position that having these records available is essential to the continued growth of collections available through catalogues. These records allow librarians to make titles available to users in short order, in many cases making titles available much sooner than if the record had to be created in-house. Why, then, do we need to discuss the outsourcing of library metadata and indexing? If there is a direct benefit to the availability of MARC records, why is there a need to examine the source of those records when received from vendors?

To assume that the only metadata libraries receive from vendors is in the form of MARC records is to take a very narrow, singular view on the rich metadata now available in online catalogues. The following sections of this chapter will introduce the depth of rich metadata and indexing that is available beyond online catalogues. Specifically, web-scale discovery services that aggregate, index and disseminate large quantities of information such as full text articles, summaries and abstracts will be examined. This chapter will then discuss the potential risks associated with complete reliance on vendors for these services.

The increasing reliance on vendors in providing metadata and indexing services requires examination. In particular, it is necessary to identify and examine the issues that arise when vendors who provide both metadata and discovery layers do not share their data with another discovery vendor.

Library discovery layers

Library discovery layers are 'interactive, collaborative library catalogues that are defined by their intuitive interfaces that often allow users to search the library's holdings, additional data sources, and user generated information' (Tarulli, 2012, 15). These catalogues display reviews on titles, suggested read-alikes, user and vendor generated tags, and ranked results. Discovery layers may also provide scrolling cover art, reading lists and faceted navigation. Faceted navigation is often exhibited in a sidebar wherein users can narrow their search by subjects (found in the MARC records), as well as reading levels, age, collection, circulation statistics or format. Faceted navigation relies on rich metadata and indexing, and it is a common feature in well used commercial sites such as Amazon, eBay and other online marketplaces.

When a library management team or librarian chooses to implement a discovery layer for their catalogue, there are numerous factors to consider. Realistically and practically, many of those considerations focus on the front end, which deals with patron perception. For example, is the discovery layer user-friendly and intuitive? Does it look and feel like the website resource users have come to expect from a web resource? Does it function well? Is it attractive? These features and offerings are uppermost in the minds of the decision makers because, in the end, the patrons and their reaction to the new face of the catalogue provides immediate feedback and buy-in into the new catalogue. Next, decision makers tend to focus on the vendors: are they reputable? What are they offering today, and what will the product offer in the future? Are they easy to deal with and reliable, or difficult to contact? What type of product support do they offer? And, of course, what is the cost estimate, today and projected into the future? At the time of the purchase there is rarely any emphasis placed on metadata.

In the scenario set out at the beginning of this chapter, you were introduced to the individual librarian, wearing multiple hats, and performing numerous duties throughout the day. In a larger library, the duties may be spread out, but only a small group, department or librarian is responsible for the actual creation or purchase of metadata that sits behind the discovery layer. Often that librarian is the head of the cataloguing department, or part of a technical services team responsible for maintaining the MARC records for the catalogue. While the information-technology staff understand the importance of metadata, their emphasis is often on how the product works, and its implementation and support processes. A metadata librarian believes it is important to identify how existing metadata records, MARC records and outsourced metadata will work in a discovery layer environment.

Let us take a look at one piece of the metadata pie: MARC records. One of the challenges with MARC records in a library is the shift from content on a card catalogue into MARC format. Many libraries with older collections have minimal, simplified records transferred from card catalogue data that do not reflect the rich bibliographic records created in our age of technology. When a discovery layer is placed over a catalogue, or integrated with a catalogue, these inconsistencies in data become glaringly and unattractively noticeable. This is often the first problem identified by patrons, but the last identified when purchasing a discovery layer. For example, if information in a MARC field that identifies a library item's format is incorrect, it becomes immediately obvious in a feature-rich discovery layer. Items might also become undiscoverable or buried deep within the results.

The reason for discussing MARC records within the larger context of discovery services is to emphasize the importance of metadata in discovery layers, and yet the shortcoming on our part, as decision makers, is to realize the significant impact that metadata has in the initial and ongoing success of the discovery layers. If decision makers do not have experience with, or a knowledge of, metadata, and focus almost exclusively on front-end functionality, unexpected problems arise. Many frontline librarians and management team members have a depth of knowledge regarding patron needs and frontline service requirements: they are experts in identifying successful patron perception, services and programming. Our entire profession, however, is not very successful in educating our professionals in the function of library catalogues or online discovery services, in particular, *how* and *why* they continue to work. Catalogues work because a team of professionals, such as metadata and cataloguing staff and vendors, continues to generate rich metadata that originates with data creation, and results in successfully retrieved user-generated or harvested data. This data is organized in keeping with practices that allow seamless discovery of information in what often reflects the same features we take for granted in commercial websites. Perhaps it is because the metadata has always appeared to be present that we do not consider what would happen if it is not present, if we cannot make it present, or if vendors are not willing to provide it.

Let us once again revisit the sole librarian introduced at the beginning of this chapter. Imagine that he or she is in a position to purchase a discovery layer. Until this point, the catalogue has provided vendor-created bibliographic records. If the record does not exist, the librarian simply finds another source. This source could be the Library of Congress or any one of a number of local or national libraries. In the end, the source from which the librarian obtains the record or bibliographic is not essential, as long as the record is available. The real disruption to workflow is in the time required to create an original MARC record. What happens, however, when the rich metadata records we have come to expect from discovery layers, with reviews, ratings, read-alikes, recommendations, and many other facets, are not available or provided by a vendor? Further, vendors who create this rich metadata may not be willing to share their metadata with a discovery layer competitor. We now have a librarian who has purchased an interactive, user-friendly discovery layer that more closely resembles a beautifully wrapped box that is empty – and no one is willing to put in a present item worthy of that beautifully wrapped box. What is its value now?

While contemplating the problems that arise when we unintentionally ignore the complex matters of metadata behind the discovery layers of catalogues, let us proceed to an even larger and profession-wide examination involving aggregate index web-scale discovery services.

Discovery layers beyond the catalogue

Beyond the catalogue lies a new discovery layer with which librarians, educators, professors, students and patrons have increasingly become familiar: the aggregate index discovery interface. Professional librarians are most familiar with aggregate index discovery interfaces, also called consolidated indexes, web-scale discovery services or search discovery layers, as they relate to vendor products offered by OCLC (WorldCat Local[1]), EBSCO (Summon[2]) and Ex Libris (Primo Central[3]).

The reason for listing the big name vendors when discussing aggregate indexing services is because they have been in a state of competition since their inception. Indeed, EBSCO and Serials Solutions are in such a state of competition that it has bordered on insult. The competition, which we can playfully call a battle, significantly heated up between EBSCO and Serials Solutions resulting in a showdown in 2010, likened to the gunfight at the O.K. Corral. More on that later. Before discussing vendors and competition, however, it is important to have a strong understanding of search discovery services as they relate to aggregate indexing beyond the library catalogue and local collection.

Discovery services: an idea is born

Faced with an ever-increasing amount of electronic resources flooding libraries with new databases, librarians struggle to organize these databases for their users. How do you flow from one interface to another? How do you keep users interested in your databases, searching each database individually, when Google is just a click away? Literally, one search box and one click away. First, we introduced our users to federated searching, which provided a single search to link across multiple databases, which returned a list of citations. As our expertise and experience grew, so did our systems. The second generation of search aggregators, the integrated library system, enhanced the federated searching experience with user-friendly interfaces and early generation discovery tools. Our efforts continued to be one step behind Google and user-expectations, however, and our systems continued to evolve. The new discovery tool, the third generation, is similar to Google in look and feel, and is by far the most powerful and complex information retrieval system. As Dan Tonkery states, 'the beauty of these third-generation systems is a single point of access to a range of library materials. This is finally a local

Google-like application to attract library users' (Tonkery, 2011, 20). Indeed, it is a thing of beauty; at least, it is in theory. Marshall Breeding (2011) observes, 'One of the strategies behind these products is the creation of massive consolidated indexes created out of citation metadata or the full text of articles harvested from the publishers and providers of content to libraries.' Breeding (2011) states further that 'this model of discovery creates an index spanning all types of library content that can provide fast retrieval results'. Indeed, with libraries willing to spend the majority of their budgets on these aggregators, the promise and potential of these systems is recognized by all. But how are they structured?

While the National Information Standards Organization (NISO) has begun to create and finalize a standardized and accepted vocabulary of terms for these discovery systems in a recent 2015 report (Breeding, 2015), I will be basing the descriptions herein on Athena Hoeppner's article 'The Ins and Outs of Evaluating Web-Scale Discovery Services' (Hoeppner, 2012). An examination of aggregated index discovery layers or discovery service solutions reveals a basic, three-tiered structure. First, there is the tool as a whole entity: this is where the largest amount of name variations exists. These services are increasingly called web-scale discovery within the library profession. In its 2015 white paper *The Future of Library Resource Discovery*, NISO appears to prefer the more generic and applicable terms simply 'discovery' or 'discovery services' (Breeding, 2015). These services continue to be referred to as discovery layers, however, taken from the original next generation catalogue terminology, as well as aggregated index discovery layers. Whichever term you or your library choose to use, a web-scale discovery service represents a 'pre-harvested central index coupled with a richly featured discovery layer providing single search across a library's local, open access and subscription collections' (Hoeppner, 2012, 8).

These discovery services comprise two elements, the central index and the discovery layer. The central index, ultimately a powerful and an enormous aggregator of resources, includes the following features:

- full text and citations from publishers
- full text and metadata from open source collections
- full text, abstracting and indexing from aggregators and subscription databases
- MARC records from library catalogues (Hoeppner, 2012).

Fulfilling their promise of a Google-like experience, discovery services rely heavily on the metadata descriptions in central indexes. If the indexing of these resources is compromised, the metadata is unavailable, or bias is entered into the algorithms to favour certain resources over others; the end result is one of mistrust, lack of transparency and frustration. The central index is the cause of much debate and heavy competition among vendors.

It is important to delve into a deeper examination of the central index to understand why it is of such value to vendors, indexing and abstracting services, publishers and librarians. The size of central indexes is difficult to grasp; in fact, Hoeppner states that 'trying to pin down and compare the exact size and shape of each central index is an exercise in frustration' (Hoeppner, 2012, 9). Indeed, with a healthy dose of appreciation for the size of an index, it is easier to understand central indexes with respect to content, the richness of their metadata, and the types of items in which are included.

Central indexes may include as little or as much metadata as a library and vendor choose when entering into a licensing agreement. Sometimes, decision makers in a library will choose to purchase more resources than they display, limiting how or when certain databases or information is displayed. Others will display all of their information together, allowing a central index to organize a complete metadata set. A central index, for example, may include some or all of the following:

- *Library supplied or created data*: This includes MARC records from the library catalogue, and additional metadata generated or maintained by the library for access to local collections or resources. This often includes digitized collections, archival collections or local content that the library has identified of value in its online retrieval practices.
- *Open access and public domain data*: This includes data from open access sources that may provide access to full text content, online public access resources and citation information.
- *Publisher metadata and full text*: Included here are author or publisher supplied content, such as citation information, abstracts and keywords. If a library has the rights to the content, full text articles and chapters may also be available; otherwise, this metadata is only searchable but cannot be displayed.
- *Web-scale discovery-licensed material*: Considered the heart of the central index, the web-scale discovery-licensed material is aggregated content from numerous information sources. This is the material to which vendors aggressively seek agreements and access rights to index, in whole or in part. The scope of access to information is based on the types of

agreements vendors make with publishers and authors.

- *Mutually licensed content*: This content can be viewed and provided through the central index, as well as independently through the library website. Generally, this includes subscription databases that the library has licensed independently, but which the central index also includes.

Hoeppner, 2012

The final element of a discovery service is the discovery layer. Discovery layers are the end-user interface and take their name from the original next generation catalogues such as Innovative Interfaces Encore[4] or ProQuest's AquaBrowser.[5] As discussed in the beginning of this chapter, discovery layers offer facets and refinement tools, single searches across the central index, relevancy-ranked results, end-user features, and connections to full text articles and enriched content.

While the discovery layer and the central index can be licensed from a single vendor, which would comprise one service, a variety of discovery layers can also be used to search the central indexes of vendors, such as Serials Solutions and EBSCO. This becomes an important consideration when a library has already invested significant resources into purchasing and implementing a next generation discovery layer for their existing library catalogue and subscription databases. These libraries are often seeking additional content and resources, but they are not in a position to afford the expense of implementing another interface to replace their recently purchased and user-approved existing discovery layer. We therefore have the overarching discovery service, which comprises a free-standing central index, and a free-standing discovery layer. This should result in a straightforward approach of choosing the best user-interface, and combining it with the most appropriate central index to serve the library's needs; however, this approach is anything but straightforward.

When problems arise

The richness of the metadata and promise of the central index within discovery services is exciting. In our profession there is a recognized value and benefit in finding a way to compete with Google for providing the organized dissemination and discovery of information. With a service that requires so many levels of information, provided by numerous information creators, aggregators, indexers, investors, service providers and disseminators (the list can go on and on), however, it is of no surprise that there have been, and continue to be, concerns over sharing the information, making some or all of the information available, and the level of transparency regarding how these central indexes function (Hoeppner, 2012; Kelley, 2012, 2013).

As we move into an examination of the factors surrounding discovery services, it is important to understand that the factors that arise for librarians and, ultimately, the end-user stem directly from the real competition and threat, perhaps somewhat perceived, among vendors, publishers, abstractors and indexers involved in the creation and dissemination of central indexes. It is with this in mind that the issues of metadata for central indexes and discovery services will be discussed.

A promised showdown at high noon and other vendor details

It is necessary to provide an introduction into the competitors and stakeholders of discovery services before discussing the actual concerns facing librarians. A short discussion is included to fully understand the issues that arise when metadata is purposely hidden, hoarded or grudgingly shared. So, while a discussion of concerns might appear to be the logical choice for the next topic of discussion, it cannot be fully understood until some background is provided on the vendors.

In 2010, a series of letters was exchanged in *The Charleston Advisor* between Tim Collins, president of EBSCO Publishing, and Stan Sorenson, vice president of product management and marketing at Serials Solutions. The letter exchange was sparked by comments that Jane Burke, vice president of ProQuest, the parent company of Serials Solutions, made about EBSCO's Discovery Service (EDS). During Burke's interview, EBSCO identified several direct and indirect comments about its competing product, EDS, as misleading and false. Burke's comments included the statements 'unlike some of our competitors, we are unbiased in our treatment of content' and 'we're seeing other new services – EDS and Primo Central, for example – repurposing existing products to attempt to do what Summon does' (Brunning and Machovec, 2010). Collins (EBSCO) and Nancy Dushkin (Ex Libris Corporate VP), both indicated that Burke's assertions were 'faulty', and that there were many 'inaccurate assumptions' (Rapp, 2010, 14). Whether intentional or the result of a bad choice of phrasing, this interview created a public exchange of letters that escalated into a challenge for the two companies to 'meet anywhere, anytime, to settle the issue' (Tonkery, 2011, 20). In particular, the meeting was to discuss the merits, strengths and weaknesses of each product so that customers could make the final decision. It was decided that the showdown, cheekily likened to the gunfight at the O.K. Corral in Tombstone, Arizona Territory, would take place at the 30th

Annual Charleston Conference. The expectation was that the winner would take all or, at least, the clear winner of the debate would walk away with librarians rushing to sign agreements for its discovery service. By all accounts, it was a draw.

According to Tonkery (2011), with only 45 minutes allotted for the debate, there was not enough time to delve into a proper discussion or address any significant issues. Almost as important, given the limited time, the audience participation that should have driven at least part of the discussion was missing. And finally, while EBSCO and Serials Solutions are heavy hitters in this industry, Ex Libris is also a major player – and one that was not invited to take part in the discussion. Despite the lack of a clear winner, the stage was set for animosity and, clearly, a battle line was drawn in the competition for metadata as well as customers.

It has not been an easy road for any of the vendors. In 2009, EBSCO and Ex Libris entered into an agreement for EBSCO to provide citation data from EBSCOhost. When EBSCO released its new discovery service EDS, it discontinued making its metadata available to Ex Libris because the latter's product, Primo Central, was a direct competitor. EBSCO had weighed the advantages of providing one of its direct competitors with its own content, and decided that walking away from the agreement would be in EBSCO's best interest. This was not in the best interest of Ex Libris or its customers, however (Breeding, 2011). Ex Libris was left to build its own relationships and partnerships with smaller content providers, while libraries waited. While Breeding (2011) indicates that the loss of EBSCO's content was a 'short-term' disruption to Primo Central's service, it does need to be recognized that buying content through a large, single package is much more helpful than building co-operative arrangements individually with smaller aggregated databases, and directly with publishers.

Vendors aggressively pursue content providers to contribute data for indexing within their discovery service so that they can boast having the richest and most complete metadata for their users. Many of these agreements indicate that full text can be searched and retrieved in only one discovery service, while other discovery services will be provided with citation information. Other agreements are strategically placed to allow maximum exposure of discovery for publishers and the creators of content. This often means that the central index is 'created out of citation metadata or the full text articles harvested' that not only provides the end-user with faster results but continues to allow a publisher of the electronic content greater exposure while retaining control over the content (Breeding, 2011). The degree to which this is achieved depends on the level of co-operation between the vendors and the producers of the content.

The librarian and the end-user: navigating through a lack of transparency

What does all of this mean for the librarian and the end-user? With the heated competition among vendors, how can librarians know what they are purchasing or which vendor's product is best suited for their end-users? As with all products, we can discuss the need to evaluate user needs, and to research user requirements and institutional mandates. Let us assume, however, that an examination into what is needed has been determined and that a library is ready to move forward to evaluate discovery tools and their metadata. Perhaps the best place to begin our discussion is with the showdown between EBSCO and Serials Solutions. As stated previously, the 45-minute debate between the two vendors did not allow time for a meaningful discussion and to address any significant issues in detail. With limited audience participation, librarians were not able to ask questions or receive answers that would meet their needs: what, then, did they walk away with? According to Tonkery (2011), there were three key takeaways from the debate: content, the quality of indexing, and integration and support.

Content and coverage

With respect to content, we might expect that each vendor boasts having the largest amount of content, and that it aggregates the richest amount of resources with the largest amount of journals and metadata. During the debate, however, Serials Solutions did not refute EBSCO's claim that it had the largest amount of content (Tonkery, 2011). Should this be the measure of quality or the deciding factor in purchasing a discovery service? Not necessarily: more content is not necessarily better. In this case, the question of content is not a statement about the quality of EDS. We could, for the sake of argument, create a mock vendor called Questing, which offers a significantly larger collection of journals and metadata than any of our existing vendors. Would Questing then be the vendor of choice among librarians? It should not. What librarians need to question, regardless of the amount of data, is the quality of the data.

Before we move on to the quality of the data, however, there is another issue that arises when vendors advertise large numbers of agreements, journals, full text articles and other content. Often, librarians need specific databases and ask the vendor if the index includes that database. As Hoeppner indicates, 'some databases do not supply metadata to any of the WSD services' (Hoeppner,

2012, 10). SciFinder Scholar (https://scifinder.cas.org) is an example of such a database. In other cases, a database will only be indexed in one vendor's discovery service, but not another; this is when a lack of transparency exists. Although a journal might not be included in the central index, a vendor might claim that a certain percentage of the journal does exist in the index. How can they do this? Even without the database and access to the full text articles, 'basic, citation-level metadata for many of the articles' still exists (Hoeppner, 2012, 10). Using this metadata, the citation-level content is added to the central index, providing end-users with information on the article in that journal, but not providing the richness or full text availability another vendor could offer. Vendors take full advantage of this metadata and often include it in their list of journals when offering their product to customers. Unfortunately, this puts the end-user at a disadvantage. Hoeppner states 'the coverage may miss two aspects of the database. First, titles that were formerly covered by the database may or may not be in the central index. And, second, subject descriptors, abstracts, and other value-added metadata that was created by the indexer will not be in the central index' (Hoeppner, 2012, 10).

There is another issue at play here. If all vendors claim to have the same content, but some hold licensing agreements with publishers for the full metadata, while others have simply mined the citation information, is it possible for librarians to determine fully what they are purchasing? Awareness might be the greatest tool and, even then, it might not be possible to comb through a list of thousands, or even tens of thousands of titles and content to determine exactly what is being offered. This lack of transparency and market standardization for claiming content will be discussed at the end of this chapter.

The quality of data

Having high quality data does not necessarily mean it can be found, or that it is organized in a meaningful or logical system that allows for discovery. According to Tonkery, 'having great content is good, but the depth and breadth of indexing is also important' (Tonkery, 2011, 20). Complex and thorough indexing is essential for the discovery of full text articles, citations and abstracts. Identifying key concepts, creating vocabulary lists and metadata mapping, as well as building a logical structure to organize and describe the information, eases all aspects of discovery. The structure of these indexes is then strengthened by the discovery layer or interface. It is here, at the interface level, that the librarian or end-user may ultimately decide on the value or success of a vendor's discovery service. In the end, comfort level and perceived success are likely two key decision factors in the choice of a discovery layer. If the discovery layer has a strong search engine, is intuitive, and retrieves relevant results quickly, it will likely lead to the vendor of choice for a library.

How do we determine the quality of the data and its content? Is quality related to the number of items indexed? Does it pertain to the recall and perceived success of the results? Or, is it the strength of the indexing, controlled vocabularies, mapping and application of information organization that determines the quality? Publishers, indexers, authors and vendors all have different methods for organizing this data and describing the content. How and when does this process become identified as successful? In truth, discovery layers may be the only option end-users have to judge the success of the index and the quality of data. If the search consistently retrieves relevant information with ease, a user may confidently say that the quality of data is exceptional.

Integration and vendor support

The final takeaway is identifying the work that is required in installing a new discovery system, and the support the vendor provides during and after installation. There are considerations and decisions that librarians must make in determining the level of support they need. Will this be a completely new discovery layer that replaces the existing overlay to the catalogue and local resources? Will the central index need to integrate with an existing discovery layer? Is the library willing to install a completely new discovery service? No matter which option is chosen, one must also consider the library's existing content: MARC records, e-resources and other local, and online content. While the vendor's central index will already be built, how will it integrate with existing library content? From the discussion at the beginning of this chapter, you will remember that a common practice in choosing a discovery layer is based on determining the front end, user related experiences, rather than on how well it integrates with the existing library data. If this practice continues with the purchase of a discovery service, what are the implications? Undiscoverable bibliographic records? Forgotten local databases and content? Will a vendor be willing to custom-index this material; if so, how will this be performed, and what is the internal cost to the library and the staff (Tonkery, 2011)? This is a significant matter to consider, when well over 80% of library budgets may be invested in discovery tools. If local content is not indexed properly, or the existing metadata is sub-standard, it is questionable whether a central index can successfully include a library's existing content. Even if the vendor agrees to index this content, without knowing the vendor's indexing practices, there is no indication that this indexing will be successful.

Discoverability and transparency in ranked results

The discoverability of local content is a concern when examining search results and relevancy ranking. Local content must be properly indexed and this usually means custom-created by the vendor to properly align with the central index. 'To best serve the library, the central index should align with both the library's available content (the books, databases, and full text), and the approach to research appropriate for its users' (Hoeppner, 2012, 9). A consideration that must be made after insuring that local library content will be properly indexed is the method by which results are retrieved and ranked. It is important that the ranking method used for a search is transparent and relevant. Without a transparent process, librarians are left wondering how or if the index is weighted in favour of certain metadata contributors, publishers or authors. Vendors have hesitated to share their indexing and retrieval processes in an effort to safeguard their expertise from their competitor; unfortunately, this is not beneficial for the end-user.

Librarians are often left to wonder if vendors intentionally bury library content, local subscriptions and databases, or if it is a matter of inconsistent indexing practices. Without standards, and without a transparent process by which librarians can determine how information is organized and retrieved, this practice will continue to be questioned. Indeed, when the element of a discovery layer is added to this process, it is often easier, albeit more costly, to simply purchase the entire discovery service from one vendor, rather than navigate the vast amount of metadata and inconsistencies that may arise from attempting to integrate one vendor's discovery layer with another's central index.

Standardization

Many of the matters identified can be collectively attributed to one issue: lack of standardization. With a standardized process, librarians could determine the discovery service that best serves their community and determine what they are in fact purchasing. Standardization is an overarching umbrella that should include transparency of indexing practices, full disclosure about the types and availability of content, ranked relevancy methods used, and degree of integration with multiple vendor products. The development and implementation of standardized processes may assist in holding vendors to a higher level of accountability and compatibility. Increasingly, librarians and information professionals are becoming less tolerant of the lack of co-operation among vendors; this type of co-operation should be viewed as beneficial to libraries, as well as vendors and publishers. As Breeding (2011) points out,

> When a content provider opts out of making their materials available to discovery products for indexing, it causes problems for libraries that depend on discovery systems. ... It's mutually advantageous to both publishers and discovery providers to cooperate, since it both increases the effectiveness of the discovery products and improves the value of the content for libraries as it makes that content more easily available to their users.

This lack of co-operation can be demonstrated by many examples and scenarios. Two of the most common are expressed here. The first is when a library prefers one discovery system, but another vendor's content. Vendors do not help competing vendors populate their discovery products, especially if each has its own central index (content) and discovery system (Kelley, 2013). As a result, 'a library may subscribe to EBSCO host content ... but if it chooses Serials Solutions' Summon or Ex Libris Primo as its discovery layer, then the discoverability of that EBSCO content is going to be complicated' (Kelley, 2013). This does not sit well with librarians: many feel that they should be able to display their purchased content in whatever discovery layer they choose, and that they should be able to find this content (Kelley, 2013).

Other librarians fear that when they purchase content, or a packaged deal from vendors, content can be pulled or withdrawn at any time by a vendor, publisher or author, leaving a library scrambling for resources and content to provide to their users. This was demonstrated publicly when EBSCO discontinued making its content available to Ex Libris' Primo Central discovery service. Libraries were left without promised resources until Ex Libris could build the same content through individual publishers, authors and various content aggregators. Breeding (2011) introduces an option that has not been practised by librarians to help provide security regarding these two concerns. While we often ask for licensing agreements from content providers or other vendors who support our library services, we have not introduced or imposed:

> requirements that vendors make content available to the discovery services provider of [our] choice for the sole purpose of indexing.
> ... There seems to be a broader acceptance of content providers to work with discovery systems, making it part of the license terms will help close the gap on the content not currently supported in this important genre of library software.
>
> Breeding, 2011

What librarians can do without standardization

Hoeppner (2012) identifies four key factors that librarians should consider when purchasing content from a vendor. They summarize many of the issues that have been identified earlier in this chapter:

- mutually licensed content
- item types
- abstracting and indexing content
- full text indexing.

How the discovery service will be used should be considered; this includes the indexed content being purchased as well as the discovery layer. Keeping this in mind when evaluating a discovery service, a librarian must determine if that service will expose all of the rich metadata from the vendor's central index, as well as the subscriptions purchased separately by the library. Will the discovery service be able to index all of the content, sort the content, and then retrieve the mutually licensed material, or will the vendor's central index take priority? An additional consideration is the number of citations or abstracts included in the vendor's discovery service or any undesirable item types. What are you looking to purchase? What does your library need? If a library is seeking to offer primarily full text articles to their users, this must be made clear to the vendor. Item types that are not necessary or wanted can influence the usefulness and success of a discovery service. Given our previous discussion about the lack of transparency in the lists that vendors often provide regarding aggregated and licensed content, this question should be asked directly and warrant an explicit answer.

In relation to the two previous points, a librarian or purchaser of a discovery service should also seek to understand if content from specialized indexing is searchable. Can specific journals be searched within the index? What about narrowing by subject? Or by content or item-type? While some of these questions may appear to be common sense, they need to be asked and answered to ensure that the library meets the demands of the users, and its mandate to support research, curriculum and general discoverability.

Finally, when deciding on a discovery service that suits the needs of a specific library or user group, we should ask the vendor 'does the central index include the backfiles for journals and have searchable full text for a variety of sources?' (Hoeppner, 2012, 39).

NISO and the future

With a feeling that nothing is secure, that we do not have a clear idea of what we are buying, or if it will be discontinued tomorrow, should we give up? Should we shrug our shoulders and continue to spend 80% of our budgets on unstable discovery services, while we cross our fingers and hope for the best? The future is not so bleak. The major vendors in our industry are aware of our problems and concerns. These vendors have been working and building relationships with us for years, if not decades. They want to serve us and want our business, and have been dealing with growing pains. Discovery services that deal with the level and magnitude of metadata with which we now operate are relatively new, and we are more savvy and demanding than perhaps we have been in the past. Vendors are learning from their mistakes and, as a profession, we now have some strong allies on our side, the largest being the NISO.

NISO identified the struggles felt in the information world regarding discovery services, having watched their growth and development since 2009. As a result, NISO created a working group and initiative aptly called the Open Discovery Initiative (ODI), which 'aims to facilitate progress through the exploration of relevant issues and the development of recommended practices for the current generation of library discovery services based on index search' (NISO, 2013). In particular, the focus of this initiative is on facilitating the transparency relating to content coverage, and recommending a standard process or consistency regarding the methods by which this content is exchanged or shared. Acknowledging the profession's various preferences for discovery layers, the initiative by NISO clearly states that their exploration into a need for transparency and standardization does not include discovery layers, but focuses directly on content coverage of vendors' central indexes, indexing practices, and the successful sharing and discoverability of metadata.

If we had listened carefully, we likely would have heard a collective sigh of relief when the working group was created, and then again when it released its first report in 2013, *Open Discovery Initiative: promoting transparency in discovery*, for comments and feedback (NISO, 2013). Finally, a legitimate working group was formed under the well respected NISO to address many of the concerns examined in this chapter. In February 2015, the working group released a white paper, authored by Marshall Breeding, called *The Future of Library Resource Discovery* (Breeding, 2015). It was the document our profession had been eagerly awaiting, written by a well respected peer to which information professionals and vendors can look for guidelines into the practice of discovery services, content indexing and sharing.

And ultimately, we start to see the sun shine as, with excitement this past summer 2015, EBSCO decided to rebuild its relationship with Ex Libris, signing an agreement for collaboration in July of 2015. The agreement focuses on optimizing the experience of library patrons who are using Ex Libris solutions to access full text content hosted on the EBSCOhost platform, and to seek additional opportunities to collaborate (EBSCO, 2015). However, this was not the first move on EBSCO's part to become more transparent and co-operative. Several months after NISO's ODI Working Group released its first report, EBSCO decided to make its metadata available to third-party discovery services. In particular, it is not only attempting to make its metadata available, but has publicly declared that it is committed to providing assistance with linking technology to support discoverability of this content within third-part discovery services. In an interview with *Library Journal*, Sam Brooks, executive vice president for EBSCO Information Services, stated that while the choice was difficult, the company hopes that 'this compromise [will] result in our being able to establish new partnerships that [will] benefit us, our partners, and our customers' (Matt, 2014).

While still in its infancy, NISO's involvement in discovery service practices, together with a few years' experience on our part, and that of the vendors, suggests that we will be able to move forward and address the many concerns that began in 2009, and which have become extremely frustrating and problematic within the last few years. Let us hope the pendulum continues to gain momentum, and that we continue to hear about, and experience, further transparency, standardization and metadata sharing across vendors and platforms. This will, we hope, be the beginning of the end of our growing pains involving discovery services. Until, perhaps, a new growing pain arises.

References

Breeding, M. (2011) Building Comprehensive Resource Discovery Platforms, *Smart Libraries Newsletter*, 4 March, www.alatechsource.org/blog/2011/03/building-comprehensive-resource-discovery-platforms.html.

Breeding, M. (2015) *The Future of Library Resource Discovery: a white paper commissioned by the NISO Discovery to Delivery (D2D) Topic Committee*, National Information Standards Organization, www.niso.org/apps/group_public/download.php/14487/future_library_resource_discovery.pdf.

Brunning, D. and Machovec, G. (2010) Interview about Summon with Jane Burke, Vice President of Serials Solutions, *Charleston Advisor*, April, www.ingentaconnect.com/content/charleston/chadv/2010/00000011/00000004/art00017?crawler=true&mimetype=application/pdf.

EBSCO (2015) *Two Industry Leaders Sign Agreement for Collaboration*, 25 July, www.ebsco.com/news-center/press-releases/two-industry-leaders-sign-agreement-for-collaboration.

Hoeppner, A. (2012) The Ins and Outs of Evaluating Web-Scale Discovery Services, *Computers in Libraries*, April, www.infotoday.com/cilmag/apr12/Hoeppner-Web-Scale-Discovery-Services.shtml.

Kelley, M. (2012) Coming into Focus: web-scale discovery services face growing need for best practices, *Library Journal*, 15 October, www.ebscohost.com/uploads/newsroom/docs/Web-Scale_Discovery_Services_-_Coming_Into_Focus_-_Library_Journal.pdf.

Kelley, M. (2013) Discovering Reciprocity, *Library Journal*, 16 April, http://lj.libraryjournal.com/2013/04/opinion/editorial/discovering-reciprocity/.

Matt, E. (2014) EBSCO Opens Metadata to Third-Party Discovery Services, *Library Journal*, 1 May, http://lj.libraryjournal.com/2014/05/technology/ebsco-opens-metadata-to-third-party-discovery-services/.

NISO (2013) *Open Discovery Initiative: promoting transparency in discovery*, National Information Standards Organization, www.niso.org/apps/group_public/download.php/14820/rp-19-2014_ODI.pdf.

Rapp, D. (2010) Competition Heats Up Discovery Marketplace, *Library Journal*, **135** (17), 14.

Tarulli, L. (2012) *The Library Catalogue as Social Space*, Libraries Unlimited.

Tonkery, D. (2011) Report from the Field: EBSCO and Serials Solutions face off over search discovery, *Information Today*, **28** (1), www.infotoday.com/IT/jan11/index.shtml.

Notes

1   www.oclc.org/worldcat.en.html.
2   www.ebscohost.com/discovery.
3   www.exlibrisgroup.com/category/PrimoOverview.
4   www.iii.com/products/sierra/encore.
5   www.proquest.com/products-services/AquaBrowser.html.

CHAPTER 7

Managing user-generated metadata in discovery systems

Louise F. Spiteri

Introduction: opening the door to user-generated content

The content of bibliographic records in library catalogues has always been strictly controlled by library staff. Metadata in these records is created in adherence to a standard scheme, usually the Anglo-American Cataloguing Rules (AACR) and, more recently, though not as extensively, the Resource Description and Access (RDA) standard. The records are contained in the Machine-Readable Cataloging (MARC) framework. The subject or 'aboutness' of works is described via standard headings, usually the Library of Congress Subject Headings (LCSH), and classified according to standards such as the Dewey Decimal Classification System or the Library of Congress Classification System. The advent of social tagging, or folksonomies, a term coined by Thomas Vander Wal (2007) in 2004, opened the discussion about how user-generated content could add value to library catalogues by enabling users to organize their personal information spaces by tagging items of interest for later retrieval, supplement existing controlled vocabularies, and create online communities of interest by using tags to connect with other users with similar research interests (Spiteri, 2006; Steele, 2009). Since 2004, user-generated content in catalogues has expanded to include ratings and reviews. This chapter will explore how user-generated content has been used in library catalogues, identify and discuss emergent themes and patterns in this use, and suggest future directions.

The metadata framework of library catalogues

Library catalogues typically contain bibliographic records whose content is created by trained professionals. The standard metadata scheme used in most catalogues for the past several decades has been the AACR. This standard describes standardized access points or elements of an item, as outlined in the International Standard Bibliographic Description:

- title and statement of responsibility area
- edition area
- material or type of resource specific area
- publication, production, distribution, etc., area
- material description area
- series area
- notes area
- resource identifier and terms of availability area (e.g., ISBN, ISSN).

IFLA, 2011

The eight elements above focus on the physical aspects of a work. The intellectual content of a work is described by the assignation of headings, derived normally from the Library of Congress (Library of Congress, n.d.); these headings can be used to describe the subject of a work, its genre, named people or entities, geographical areas or relevant periods.

AACR records are typically contained in the MARC framework (Library of Congress, 2009), which allows different computers and operating systems to read and understand the content of the bibliographic records. Elements of the bibliographic content are mapped onto corresponding MARC fields; for example field 245 contains information about the title and statement of responsibility. Headings that describe the intellectual content of the work are contained in the 600 series of MARC fields.

In 2010, the new metadata standard RDA was published to replace AACR. Although AACR had undergone modifications and revisions over the years, its design was still very much based on the card catalogue. RDA was designed for the digital world, and provides:

- a flexible framework for describing all resources (analogue and digital) that is extensible for new types of material
- data that is readily adaptable to new and emerging database structures
- data that is compatible with existing records in online library catalogues.

RDA Steering Committee, n.d.

Like their AACR counterparts, RDA records contain descriptions of the physical aspects and intellectual content of a work. RDA records are created by professionals, and can be housed in the MARC framework used in most library catalogues. The content of MARC records cannot be manipulated in any way by the end-user of the library catalogue. Typically, library professionals have sole control over the description of the physical features and intellectual content of the work.

Social features of web-scale discovery systems

Library catalogue records, be they created using AACR or RDA standards, do not typically accommodate any external metadata contributed by the end-user. Over the past decade, we have seen the rise of what are often referred to as web-scale discovery systems. These new systems contain a number of features that enhance the discovery and access features of catalogues (Han, 2012), including:

- *Faceted navigation*: Arguably the best known feature of these catalogues, faceted navigation allows the user to drill down search results by selecting facets such as format, language, subject and so forth.
- *Data harvesting*: These systems can harvest and index data from multiple sources other than the library catalogue, such as external digital repositories and article databases.
- *Participatory architecture*: Influenced by the social features of web-based services such as blogs and bookmarking sites, these new systems provide opportunities for users to contribute and share their own content via features such as tags and reviews, thus helping to make the library catalogue a virtual space that is more 'interactive, collaborative, and driven by community needs'.

Houghton-John, 2006

In this chapter, focus is placed on the social features of web-scale discovery systems, namely those that allow users to input and share their own metadata, primarily through the inclusion of tags and reviews. Additional features may include the creation of reading lists that can be shared with other users, related videos and film trailers.

Why add user content to library catalogue records?

The library catalogue has long acted as an important and fundamental medium between users and their information needs. The traditional goals and objectives of the library catalogue are to enable users to search a library's collection to find items pertaining to specific titles, authors or subjects. Today's library catalogues are competing against powerful alternatives for information discovery. Services offered by sites such as Amazon (www.amazon.com), Goodreads (www.goodreads.com) and LibraryThing (www.librarything.com) allow members to interact with the catalogue and with each other by creating and participating in discussion groups, tagging or classifying items of interest in language that reflects their needs, sharing reading, listening or viewing interests, and providing recommendations and ratings for selected items (Spiteri, 2012). These types of services serve to heighten library users' expectations of a library catalogue. In a study of online catalogues, Calhoun et al. (2009) concluded that 'the principles of usability and user-centred design might be said to have displaced the traditional principles of information organization, at least as librarians have practiced them' (59).

If the public library catalogue is to continue to be relevant to its users, it needs to move beyond its current inventory model, where all content is designed and controlled by library staff and client interaction with catalogue content is limited, to a social catalogue, where users can contribute to and interact with information and with each other (Calhoun, 2006; Fast and Campbell, 2004; Furner, 2007; Spiteri, 2009).

User-generated metadata to enhance subject analysis systems

In a typical bibliographic record, description of an item is divided into three elements: physical description, subject description, and main and added entries. The physical description identifies the physical attributes of an item, such as its title, statements of responsibility, publication date and so forth. Subject description is divided into two sections: a classification number is assigned to an item that captures the main subject content of the work, normally the Dewey Decimal Classification for public libraries, and the Library of Congress Classification for academic libraries. This classification number has traditionally served as a location device to help users find a specific item on a shelf. The second component consists of headings assigned to describe the subject content and sometimes the genre of the item. These headings are normally derived from standardized lists, most commonly the LCSH. The main and added entries collocate related entries under standardized headings for named entities, derived most commonly from the Library of Congress; for example, all works written by William Shakespeare owned by the library system can be discovered by clicking on the standardized heading for this author: **Shakespeare, William, 1564–1616**.

Over the past decade, a number of studies have examined the relationship between user-contributed tags and LCSH, and the extent to which the two systems work to provide access to the content of bibliographic items in the catalogue. The two systems are diametrically opposed to one another. In LCSH, only one standardized heading may be used to express a given topic; variant terms for that topic serve as lead-in terms to the standardized heading. So, for example, the LCSH term **motion pictures** is used to express the variant terms **films** or **movies**.

Further, LCSH provides hierarchies or controlled taxonomies of terms, so that narrower types or genres of films (e.g., **Action and adventure films**) are linked to the broader term **motion pictures**. User tags, on the other hand, share the problems inherent to all uncontrolled vocabularies, such as ambiguous headings, polysemy (the same word can have different meanings) and synonymy (different words have the same meaning). Further, user tags exist in a flat hierarchy: they lack a taxonomic structure whereby conceptually related terms are brought together, such as linking different types of films subsumed under a broader heading for films. Given the inherent differences between the two systems, can they successfully co-exist in library catalogues?

Steele (2009) argues that tagging can offer users advantages that are not offered by a traditional library classification system based on a controlled vocabulary. These systems operate on the assumption that there is a proper place for everything, and this place is determined by the professional cataloguer. In a folksonomy, however, these pre-determined hierarchies do not exist. A resource may belong in any number of places, be it a single hierarchy, or many different hierarchies, or none at all.

An examination of the LCSH heading **motion picture** highlights some of the problems that are often inherent to standardized taxonomies. The Library of Congress defines 'motion pictures' as 'a topical heading for general works about motion pictures themselves, including motion pictures as an art form, copyrighting, distribution, editing, plots, production, etc.' (Library of Congress, 2015). **Films** and **movies** are considered to be variant terms – they link to the heading **motion pictures**, but are not assigned to records to describe this topic. The term **motion pictures** is perfectly valid in its own right; in fact, it appears in the title of the Academy of Motion Pictures and Sciences (Academy of Motion Pictures and Sciences, 2015), the world's largest film-related organization, which is most closely associated with the Oscars. **Motion pictures** is not, however, the term that many, or most, people would use to search for films. The Library of Congress taxonomy for **motion pictures** shows variant uses of terms within the hierarchy; for example, it includes a number of narrower terms that contain the words **films** and **motion pictures**, e.g., **Animal films** and **Animals in motion pictures**. The term **films** appears to be used to specify the type or genre of film (what the film is), while **motion pictures** is used to specify the concept of films as a whole. From the purely classificatory point of view, one can understand this distinction, but it is not clear whether such fine distinctions would be evident to the average searcher.

Thomas, Caudle and Schmitz (2009) found that user-generated tags can play an important role in enhancing the metadata in an online catalogue by expanding the search terminology available to users. The authors conducted an evaluation of seven catalogues to examine the extent to which folksonomies would successfully complement cataloguer-supplied subject headings in library catalogues. This study examined specifically catalogues that import user tags from LibraryThing, the popular online social book cataloguing site. Their comparison of the tags and subject headings assigned to the same set of books revealed only a small cross section of common terms between the tag content and the assigned subject headings, and that almost one-third of the tags represented valid content that had not been included in the subject headings.

Kakali and Papatheodorou (2010) researched the relationship between user-generated tags and subject headings in the online catalogue at the Panteion University Library and reviewed over 500 tags in over 200 bibliographic records. The authors determined that over 90% of the tags enhanced the subject access of the records, and that the tags represented terms that are both broader and narrower than the Library of Congress headings. In some instances, the authors found that the tags provided better descriptions of the content than did the subject headings.

Content analyses of tags assigned to titles in LibraryThing and subject headings assigned to the same items have revealed that folksonomies may be especially useful in augmenting descriptions of items whose content is not adequately described in LCSH. Adler (2009) examined 20 books that covered a wide range of transgender themes, including drag, transsexuality, genderqueer and intersexuality. Adler compared the subject headings assigned to the books in WorldCat with the tags assigned to them in LibraryThing. Adler found that the Library of Congress headings and user tags differed significantly. The user tags provided several representations of gender identity and expressions, while most of these representations were absent in the Library of Congress headings in WorldCat. Adler suggests that while neither the tags nor the subject headings are perfect systems on their own, they serve to complement each other well in library catalogues, and that 'bringing users' voices into catalogs through the addition of tags might greatly enhance organization, representation, and retrieval of transgender-themed materials' (Adler, 2009, 309).

Mendes, Quiňónez-Skinner and Skaggs (2009) examined the use of LibraryThing tags in the Oviatt Library catalogue at California State University over a period of 170 days. The authors found that for every new book a user discovers using Library of Congress headings, they will discover four books using LibraryThing tags, and suggest that the addition of user-generated tags to catalogue records enhances resource discovery, for example, for those titles lacking subject headings, which is sometimes the case for works of fiction. Tags facilitated the discovery of resources by genre and, since they reflect the natural language of users, provide new paths for resource discovery.

DeZelar-Tiedman (2011) compared LCSH and LibraryThing tags in the University of Minnesota online catalogue for 20th and 21st century English and American literary works. Her examination of 444 records found a considerably higher number of tags assigned to the records than subject headings. The record sampling also showed the lack of subject access for many 20th and 21st century literary works in academic library catalogues: 61% of the catalogue records in the sample had no subject headings. Conversely, only 7.1% of the 367 work records in LibraryThing had no tags.

The studies above suggest that user-generated tags can play an important role in library catalogues by providing terms that complement or supplement cataloguer-supplied subject headings. This means that user tags can provide libraries with a vocabulary that users can more easily use in their searches (Anfinnsen, Ghinea and de Cesare, 2011). Tags reflect users' language, needs and conceptions of information. Further, tags are also highly responsive to changes of user vocabularies and needs (Porter, 2011). Let us examine this more closely. I have argued elsewhere that user-generated metadata can provide us with an opportunity to ensure that our bibliographic records reflect more closely the concept of 'cultural warrant', which suggests that any knowledge organization or representational system should reflect the assumptions, values and predispositions of the culture(s) in which it exists (Spiteri, 2012). Bibliographic records should be designed with the needs of the end-user in mind; in fact, meeting these user needs is the primary principle of most information professions. The problem in the field of bibliographic description is that cataloguers often do not have a clear knowledge of user needs; further, time constraints limit the amount of customization that can be made to bibliographic records to reflect the cultural warrants of local communities. So, for example, Library of Congress headings, which are designed to reflect the needs, culture and language of the Library of Congress in the USA, may not always reflect the differing cultural needs of people who live in Canada. To illustrate, the Canadian term 'First Nations' is not an authorized heading in LCSH; it is a variant for 'Indians of North America', a term that would be considered outdated and offensive to most Canadians. User tags can provide opportunities to include content that reflects the needs of local communities, including terms in languages other than English, which is particularly important in a country like Canada, whose citizens speak a large variety of languages, with the caveat that they can be written in the Roman alphabet. So, for example, the term 'woman' could be expressed via user tags in the six languages spoken by the Iroquois Nations:[1]

- ago:nhgweh (Cayuga)
- yakonkwe (Mohawk)
- yakukwé (Oneida)
- yakökwe (Seneca)
- Akę:kweh (Tuscarora).

Even though Library of Congress headings are updated frequently, they might not always change quickly enough to reflect changes in language. Library of Congress headings are based on the principle of literary warrant: they reflect the published contents of the Library of Congress, and those institutions that are engaged in co-operative activities with the Library of Congress. Therefore new words might not appear quickly enough in the published literature to warrant their timely incorporation into the list of subject headings. User tags, on the other hand, are not bound by such strictures, and can reflect more quickly the emergence of new vocabularies. Understandably, a standardized list should avoid incorporating terms that are too colloquial and fleeting in nature, as this can result in too many updates, as well as inconsistencies in bibliographic records, since staff might not have time to make the necessary updates to subject headings. On the other hand, subject headings run the risk of becoming fossilized and outdated. User tags can provide alternatives to the Library of Congress headings that are more accessible to the user, and that can serve as suggestions for new terms to be incorporated into LCSH.

Steele (2009) argues that web content grows faster than bots can extract keywords and fit into a search engine's hierarchy. In the same manner, libraries receive content, especially electronic content, faster than it can be catalogued. The need for metadata can be alleviated by tagging; therefore one of the most important reasons libraries should consider the use of tags is for the benefits of evolution and growth.

User-generated metadata can provide de facto subject access

An interesting theme that has emerged in the literature is the use of tags to provide subject access to items to which Library of Congress headings have not been assigned. For example, traditionally libraries have not provided the same level of subject access to works of fiction as they have to non-fiction. A commonly cited reason for this lack of subject access is that the aboutness of works of fiction is often more subjective than for non-fiction (DeZelar-Tiedman, 2011). This argument might not bear close scrutiny, however, as it is not clear how or why determining the aboutness of works of non-fiction is necessarily less subjective than that of works of fiction. In my many years of teaching cataloguing and subject analysis, my students invariably mention how difficult it can be to determine and choose the subject content of works of non-fiction, for a variety of reasons, such as their knowledge of the discipline involved, the variety of topics from which to choose, particularly if a work is an edited work, the difficulty of separating the form of the work from its content, and so forth. Each of these variables can affect one's choice of appropriate headings to describe content. Perhaps rather too much is made about the ideal of non-subjective bibliographic records. The provision of unbiased catalogue records, while laudable, is rarely truly attainable in practice. Cataloguers decide what to include and exclude in a catalogue record. There have been several studies that have pointed to inherent biases in the contents (or omissions) of catalogue records (Bade, 2002; Olson, 2000, 2002; Smiraglia, 2009). Further, it is not clear to what extent neutrality and inclusivity are possible via systems such as LCSH, which may include biases and assumptions that reflect certain sociopolitical or cultural norms (Pecoskie, Spiteri and Tarulli, 2014).

DeZelar-Tiedman (2011) argues that depending on the work, settings, historical periods or characters, recurring fictional characters and genres can be relatively simple to identify for works of fiction or drama, but thematic topics can be more elusive and more challenging to determine without reading the entire work. Even then, themes such as alienation, redemption or betrayal may be open to interpretation and are rarely explicitly stated. While these are certainly valid points, they might, in fact, point to the importance of including user tags in bibliographic records of works of fiction, since while cataloguing staff assign headings based on a cursory examination of the work at hand, it is far more likely that users assign tags to an item after they have actually read or listened to it, so they could very well have a greater understanding of the aboutness and themes of the item than do the cataloguing staff.

Another emerging phenomenon is the contribution of user-generated tags to older bibliographic records. West (2013) examined 28 graphic novel titles in 75 academic library catalogues that use social tagging. Traditionally, once a title has been added to an online catalogue it is unlikely that the record would be altered unless a specific request was made, so it is very possible for older bibliographic records to have outdated Library of Congress headings, or none at all. West postulated that user tags provide a mechanism to enhance records of, and access to, older works at no cost of time or labour to the library. Of the 28 titles examined dated between 1979 and 2003, West found that there were twice as many instances of graphic novel tags (56) than genre or subject headings (24). With increasing cuts to library budgets, user tags could provide additional access to records that either lack Library of Congress subject headings, or whose headings are outdated and not reflective of current usage.

User-generated metadata provides richer bibliographic content

According to Gretchen Hoffman, librarians are often accused of using expertise to decide what is best for our users. Our cataloguing practices and legacy catalogues are a good example of this: 'although cataloging claims to focus on users, the cataloging field has generally not taken a user-centered approach in research and cataloging standards have not been developed based on an understanding of users' needs' (Hoffman, 2009, 632). Hoffman suggests that many inadequacies in bibliographic records are the result of the limited ability to customize bibliographic records, shortcomings with cataloguing software, and an emphasis on productivity and efficiency over customization of records.

The quality of the traditional catalogue record is of critical importance. Although the Library of Congress published a set of minimal-level record examples (Library of Congress, 2008), it is hard to enforce the creation of even minimal-level cataloguing records. This state of affairs results in inconsistent and incomplete records in cataloguing systems, both in the local system and in the union cataloguing system provided by OCLC (the Online Computer Library Center (Han, 2012). Calhoun et al. (2009) conducted a study for OCLC to examine user and librarian perceptions of cataloguing quality. This study found that there is a disconnection between these perceptions, which are driven by different outlooks and goals. The user identifies more with the information environment on the web, and seeks more direct access to online content. Users also want more of what OCLC calls 'enrichment data', such as tables of contents and summaries in catalogue records. The librarian, on the other hand, is more focused on the most efficient means of fulfilling work assignments. Librarians' ideas of quality cataloguing are biased towards attributes like the elimination of duplicate records and fixing MARC coding errors, which may or may not affect information retrieval on the user's end (Schultz-Jones et al., 2012).

With cutbacks to technical services staff, and our increasing reliance on vendor-provided records (including OCLC), are we providing enough subject detail to clients via the MARC records? Is minimal-level cataloguing sufficient? Do these records provide enough information to the clients? Are these records so generic as to not reflect local communities and cultures? As we continue to strip down our records in the name of economy, user-generated metadata may play an increasingly important role in library catalogues.

As has been discussed previously, assigning subject headings to works depends to a significant extent on the cataloguers' ability to understand the content of the work at hand. Cataloguers might be expected to work with items that vary greatly in subject, discipline and scope. It may be very possible that users have significantly more knowledge about particular topics and disciplines than cataloguing staff. User-generated metadata might not only serve to complement staff-chosen headings, but could actually be more accurate and relevant to the items at hand. User-generated metadata can thus serve to distribute subject expertise across many members of the library community. As a small example, I have often had occasion to note how poorly works about veganism are catalogued in academic and public libraries. 'Veganism' is often equated with 'vegetarianism' (related, but separate concepts), or no distinction is made between 'ethical veganism' (the refusal to participate in the commercialization of animals for ethical reasons), versus a 'plant-based diet', where the focus is on only abstaining from animal products for health rather than ethical reasons. Although these distinctions might seem minor, they are very important to ethical vegans, and to members of vegan communities. So, for example, the assignation of the heading 'vegan' to a cookbook that has a mix of vegan, vegetarian and animal-based recipes – which are popular in flexitarian diets – would be considered inaccurate, misleading and possibly even offensive to ethical vegans. In cases such as these, user-generated metadata could help provide a more accurate description of the subject contents of bibliographic records.

Gerolimos (2013) turns upside down the concept of user-generated metadata as a service that libraries provide to users; rather, he suggests that this metadata is, in fact, a service that users provide to libraries. Since users have become a part of the process of subject description, they now have the potential to be more than searchers or browsers of information; they can become contributors as subject experts.

User-generated metadata beyond the catalogue

The fact that web-scale discovery systems allow for access to collections beyond those contained in library catalogues expands greatly the potential contributions of user-generated metadata to providing subject access to bibliographic items. If these external sources of bibliographic information also allow for user-generated metadata, this metadata might become an essential access point. Chang and Iyer (2012, 253) explored the possibility of adding Twitter hashtags as a design feature of library catalogues:

> Twitter hashtags can blend both communication and organization by helping information professionals enhance research or reading experiences and by bringing users and resources closer together. As with other social media platforms, Twitter can be used to quickly connect people and to allow them to follow updates about each other. Alternatively, a person could connect with new people by

joining the information networks and news channels that reflect one's own interests, link to breaking news, or disseminate business updates – which may take a great deal more effort.

Chang and Iyer (2012) say that library catalogues can incorporate Twitter data streams on related topics (e.g., #metadata) to optimize third-party applications equipped with functions that include search, directory and archiving functions, and which allow analysis and visualization of Twitter hashtags used within the library catalogue environment and linking out to the richness of the Twitterverse. Library staff can use hashtags as a useful search strategy. Users can use a hashtag to connect them to a variety of useful resources that exist outside the library collection. Although Chang and Iyer focused only on Twitter, many social networking sites now share hashtags across their platforms. Let us use veganism again to illustrate this point. Social media sites that discuss vegan lifestyles and plant-based diets can be connected via common social tags, such as 'vegan', 'veganism', 'animal rights', 'animal welfare' and so forth. A search for the hashtag '#vegan', for example, produces results from Twitter, Instagram, Facebook and Tumblr, where this tag is used in common.[2]

As libraries continue to add enriched content to their bibliographic records, such as cover images, tables of contents, abstracts and external reviews, it is important that they consider whether user-generated metadata should be integrated into the MARC bibliographic records (Han, 2012). Breeding (2010) suggests that quality cataloguing for library discovery systems should convey the full range of a library's collections. The narrow scope of traditional online library catalogues often neglects individual chapter titles of books, individual article titles in periodicals, and specific items within larger collections. As mentioned previously, the MARC record is created by library staff; its contents cannot be changed or manipulated in the public interface. User-generated content appears as an additional layer that lies outside the MARC record. Therefore when tags are used in the discovery layer of a library's catalogue, they are not in any way part of the catalogue database that underlies the user-interface. If a library does wish to use tags to enhance catalogue record data directly, it might accomplish this by importing them into the MARC field 653, which is used for uncontrolled index terms. As web-scale discovery systems allow us to access and share a larger amount and variety of bibliographic content, we need to consider that rich user-generated content could be lost if it is not incorporated in the MARC record. As discovery systems and user behaviours continue to evolve, those working with catalogue data must continue to explore ways to enhance access to information resources of all kinds and to improve the user experience. Capitalizing on aggregated end-user data about resources is an important way to achieve that aim (DeZelar-Tiedman, 2011).

User-generated metadata and readers' advisory

A recent area of exploration involves the role of user-generated metadata in readers' advisory services in public libraries. In traditional readers' advisory services, knowledgeable library staff help readers with their leisure-reading needs. In most public libraries, readers' advisory models are heavily based on the traditional reference-interview structure. The conversations start with a roving readers' advisor approaching a reader within the library or a patron who approaches a readers' advisory staff member. The readers' advisory librarian generally has a list of pre-determined questions that assists in deciding which books to suggest, and when the reader leaves, the conversation is documented by a statistic, with little or no feedback or follow-up with that patron (Tarulli and Spiteri, 2012).

Hollands (2006) explores five assumptions that we make about our traditional model:

- Readers initiate or approach a readers' advisor with reading questions.
- The staff member approached will have the knowledge to answer the readers' advisor questions.
- Through our readers' advisory interviews, we gather enough information to provide good readers' advisory services.
- Time constraints do not interfere with the quality of readers' advisory services that we provide.
- The use of databases and other readers' advisor sources are easy to use while conducting face-to-face readers' advisory interviews.

The traditional readers' advisor model assumes, therefore, that readers are comfortable approaching a staff member and discussing their reading preferences. A commonly cited problem is the reluctance on the part of many readers to discuss their reading interests with librarians, possibly because of shyness, a lack of awareness that some librarians are trained to provide this type of service, a perception of librarians being intimidating or unapproachable authority figures, assumptions that a librarian of a different age, gender or culture may not relate to them, and a fear of having their reading interests dismissed or judged.

Reading preferences can be very personal. Library discovery systems can offer important new ways to complement the traditional readers' advisor model, which includes providing an online environment where users can establish a social space to share and discuss common reading interests. This social space provides a grassroots and democratic readers' advisor service that allows users to comment on titles read, make recommendations for future reading based on shared interests, and classify items in the catalogue with their own tags or reviews that may be more reflective of their language and needs than the formal subjects assigned by library staff. These tags and reviews can serve as added access points by which readers can search for items of interest. Librarians and library staff can interact with users, learn more about their needs, and become part of the online community, while at the same time compile recommended reading lists and make purchasing decisions based on the reviews and recommendations made in the catalogue by users (Pecoskie, Spiteri and Tarulli, 2014).

Pecoskie, Spiteri and Tarulli (2014) conducted a content analysis of Library of Congress, user tags and user reviews contained in the bibliographic records for 22 fiction titles in 43 Canadian public library catalogues that allow for the addition of user-generated metadata. This study found that user tags place a greater emphasis on the topic of a book, or what could be called the subject of the work. Subject headings, on the other hand, emphasize the genre of the book rather than information about the book's subject, which tallies well with the point made earlier about the often inadequate subject description of works of fiction. Both user tags and reviews contained information on the tone and mood of the books, as well as of triggered memories and experiences. These findings point to the importance of user-generated metadata as a way to allow readers to express the affective aspects of a book: its emotional impact on them. Subject headings are not equipped to deal with affect, since the emphasis of cataloguing has traditionally been on describing the more neutral components of a work, such as locations, periods and topics. User-generated metadata can serve to express important aspects of a work that cannot always be expressed easily by subject headings. Where cataloguers want an objective stance on what the title conveys, users want to provide a complete picture of the title, including its subject and emotional impact, and their reading experience. User-generated metadata can thus serve to add valuable additional information to a bibliographic record about the affective or emotional impact of a book. Tagging, in particular, allows for the broader expansion of a readership community, where the individual user, through those tag connections, may share reading interests with others. User-generated reviews allow for a similar level of expansion, since users can click on the associated username to see other titles, tags and reviews with which this name is associated. Pecoskie and Spiteri are continuing their analysis of the user reviews obtained from these records to create taxonomies of emotions, tones and associations that readers associate with these titles. These taxonomies could serve as useful tools for readers' advisor librarians to help readers select items to read, as well as further facets by which searchers could narrow the focus of their search in a library catalogue, for example, by allowing them to select books based on emotions and tones, or to search for books that are sad and cerebral.

Conclusion

Over the past decade, a number of developments have occurred in the incorporation of user-contributed metadata in library catalogues. The ability to organize personal information spaces in library catalogues has not been discussed very much over the past decade, and is not necessarily a common or popular feature in most web-scale discovery systems. Discovery layers such as BiblioCommons (www.bibliocommons.com), for example, do allow users to add items to their wish lists, but the use of this type of feature has not been studied extensively. Further, this wish list feature appears thus far to be restricted to compiling items only from within the library catalogue. If web-scale discovery services are expanded to provide access to bibliographic items indexed across a variety of sources, features that allow users to organize and categorize their personalized lists of items in the library catalogue, citations from external databases, external web pages and so forth might become increasingly important and certainly worthy of further study.

The use of social tags to supplement or complement controlled vocabularies has become an important theme over the past decade. Unlike subject headings, which are created, maintained and updated in a controlled environment, and which may reflect the cultural, social and linguistic biases of specific collections, user tags are self-moderating and inclusive. This democratic approach to indexing and retrieval offered by tags allows users to articulate their individual vocabularies and viewpoints. This lowers the cognitive barriers to participation, and creates a more inclusive environment. Folksonomies reflect users' language, needs and conceptions of information, and provide an alternative to centrally imposed, top-down systems (Porter, 2011). User tags are more responsive to changes in language and can reflect the cultural warrant of local communities. Gerolimos points out that a combination of natural and controlled vocabularies is probably the most effective way for users to access and retrieve bibliographic items. User tags and Library of Congress provide this type of hybrid model, which combines 'the professionalism and expertise of librarians with the raw power of the masses to describe the content of the documents and the resources that a library has to offer' (Gerolimos, 2013, 47).

The creation of online communities of interest via user-generated metadata has not yet reached its full potential. Tarulli and Spiteri (2012) have posited that library discovery systems can promote user interaction with staff. Web-scale discovery systems provide not only the social features sought by many of our community members, but also access to all of our collections, many of which are now online. Web-scale discovery systems can extend access to beyond the collection, by linking users to recorded author readings or programmes, programme announcements, special events within the library, and links into the greater community, which could aid in the creation of community spaces. Anfinnsen, Ghinea and de Cesare suggest that it is possible for catalogues to empower library users, and make them more active participants within the community served by the library, by providing them with the means to use their own vocaublary to describe the publications they read (Anfinnsen, Ghinea and de Cesare, 2011, 64). Although these authors focus on books, their comments could easily be extrapolated to apply also to items that users can watch or listen to.

As we have seen, not all library materials are assigned sufficiently detailed or relevant subject headings, particularly works of fiction. User-generated metadata could, in fact, provide the best access to the content of these materials. Further, older bibliographic records might contain outdated subject headings, thereby potentially raising the importance and relevance of user-assigned tags. With shrinking library budgets, and an increased reliance on vendor-supplied records, bibliographic content in library catalogues could constitute a level that is too minimal to meet the needs of users. Minimal-level catalogue records run contrary to users' increasing demand for richer content. User-generated metadata could provide valuable enriched content that is lacking in minimal-level catalogue records. Further, end-users might have greater expertise in certain subjects than the cataloguing staff, and may thus be in a better position to assign descriptors that reflect accurately the subject of bibliographic items. Finally, since users have likely read, watched or listened to the items they tag or review, which is normally not the case for cataloguing staff, user content could be more comprehensive and accurate than the assigned subject headings.

As we continue to explore the possibilities that web-scale discovery systems present in expanding search to include items both within and without library catalogues, user-generated metadata can become valuable sources of access points to link bibliographic records across collections. As we have seen, this expanded scope of web-scale discovery systems may require a new perspective into the integration of user-generated metadata directly into the bibliographic record via, for example, the MARC format, rather than to continue to have this metadata sit outside the record, and thus not easily linkable or indexable across collections.

User-generated content in the form of tags and reviews can provide valuable insight into the tone and mood of a work, versus subject headings, which focus on more tangible aspects of work, such as genre, period and location. Since so much of reading interests are formed by affective aspects such as tone and mood, readers' advisory staff could mine this valuable data from user-generated content to enhance their reading recommendations.

Shared hashtags can serve as a powerful tool to bring together content from a variety of sources. As scholarly information is being disseminated increasingly via social media websites, there is scope for linking to hashtags in public and academic libraries. The significance and impact of adding these extra layers of discovery to the library catalogues need to be explored further, of course, but the role of hashtags in library catalogues is an intriguing idea and one worthy of further exploration.

Gerolimos (2013) suggests that the key to making user-generated metadata work for libraries is not participation, since libraries will likely not experience the level of participation that other web services have, but user willingness, which translates to the will of the few to devote some of their time to the online activities that a library offers. The concept of user motivation is an important factor that underlies the potential contributions of user-generated metadata to library catalogues. Gerolimos (2013) and Michalko (2009) suggest that not all library users might ever become too motivated or interested in participating in the process of subject description, and that this process might never become an everyday activity for the majority of users. Sites such as Amazon, IMDb (the Internet Movie Database; www.imdb.com) and Goodreads, are good examples of rich user content, which can number in the several hundred entries, or more, for any given item. Given this, it is important that we research further the role motivation plays in the creation of user-generated content in library catalogues. Are people more likely to add metadata to sites like Goodreads than they are to a library catalogue? If so, why? How do people use, perceive and interact with sites such as Goodreads in comparison to library catalogues? Do library users view the library catalogue as a social, interactive environment, or are catalogues losing ground increasingly to sites like Amazon, IMDb and Goodreads, which have vibrant communities of members who interact with each other in an exploration of shared reading and viewing interests?

References

Academy of Motion Pictures and Sciences (2015) *About,*
   www.oscars.org.

Adler, M. (2009) Transcending Library Catalogues: a comparative
   study of controlled terms in Library of Congress Subject Headings
   and user-generated tags in LibraryThing for transgender books,
   Journal of Web Librarianship, **3** (4), 309–31.

Anfinnsen, S., Ghinea, G. and de Cesare, S. (2011) Web 2.0 and
   Folksonomies in a Library Context, *International Journal of
   Information Management,* **31** (1), 63–70.

Bade, D. (2002) *The Creation and Persistence of Misinformation in Shared
   Library Catalogs: language and subject knowledge in a technological era,*
   University of Illinois at Urbana-Champaign.

Breeding, M. (2010) *Next-gen Library Catalogs,* Neal-Schuman.

Calhoun, K. (2006) *The Changing Nature of the Catalog and its Integration
   with other Discovery Tools,* Library of Congress,
   www.loc.gov/catdir/calhoun-report-final.pdf.

Calhoun, K., Cantrell, J., Gallagher, P. and Hawk, J. (2009) *Online
   Catalogs: what users and librarians want,* Online Computer Library
   Center, www.oclc.org/us/en/reports/onlinecatalogs/fullreport.pdf.

Chang, H.-C. and Iyer, H. (2012) Trends in Twitter Hashtag
   Applications: design features for value-added dimensions to
   future library catalogues, *Library Trends,* **61** (1), 248–58.

DeZelar-Tiedman, C. (2011) Exploring User-Contributed Metadata's
   Potential to Enhance Access to Literary Works: social tagging in
   academic library catalogs, *Library Resources & Technical Services,*
   55 (4), 221–33.

Fast, K. V. and Campbell, D. G. (2004) I Still Like Google: university student perceptions of searching OPACs and the web, *Proceedings of the American Society for Information Science and Technology*, **41** (1), 138–46.

Furner, J. (2007) *User Tagging of Library Resources: toward a framework for system evaluation*, paper given at World Library and Information Congress: 73rd IFLA General Conference and Council, Durban, South Africa, http://archive.ifla.org/IV/ifla73/papers/157-Furner-en.pdf.

Gerolimos, M. (2013) Tagging for Libraries: a review of the effectiveness of tagging systems for library catalogs, *Journal of Library Metadata*, **13** (1), 36–58.

Han, M.-J. (2012) New Discovery Systems and Library Bibliographic Control, *Library Trends*, **61** (1), 162–72.

Hoffman, G. L. (2009) Meeting Users' Needs in Cataloging: what is the right thing to do?, *Cataloging & Classification Quarterly*, **47** (7), 631–41.

Hollands, N. (2006) Improving the Model for Interactive Readers' Advisory Services, *Reference & User Services Quarterly*, **45** (3), 205–12, www.accessmylibrary.com/coms2/summary_0286-15531994_ITM.

Houghton-John, S. (2006) *Library 2.0 Discussion: Michael Squared*, 10 January, http://librarianinblack.net/librarianinblack/library_20_disc.

IFLA (2011) *ISBD: International Standard Bibliographic Description*, International Federation of Library Associations and Institutions, De Gruyter Saur.

Kakali, C. and Papatheodorou, C. (2010) Exploitation of Folksonomies in Subject Analysis, *Library & Information Science Research*, **32** (3), 192–202.

Library of Congress (n.d.) *Library of Congress Linked Data Service*, http://id.loc.gov.

Library of Congress (2008) *Appendix C – Minimal Level Record Examples*, www.loc.gov/marc/bibliographic/bdapndxc.html.

Library of Congress (2009) *Understanding MARC Bibliographic: machine-readable cataloging*, www.loc.gov/marc/umb.

Library of Congress (2015) *Motion Pictures*, http://id.loc.gov/authorities/subjects/sh85088084.html.

Mendes, L. H., Quiñónez-Skinner, J. and Skaggs, D. (2009) Subjecting the Catalog to Tagging, *Library Hi Tech*, **27** (1), 30–41.

Michalko, J. (2009) *Things that Happen Elswhere – user studies say*, 5 June, http://hangingtogether.org/?p=702.

Olson, H. A. (2000) Difference, Culture, and Change: the untapped potential of LCSH, *Cataloging & Classification Quarterly*, **29** (1/2), 53–71.

Olson, H. A. (2002) *The Power to Name: locating the limits of subject representation in libraries*, Kluwer Academic.

Pecoskie, J., Spiteri, L. F. and Tarulli, L. (2014) OPACs, Users, and Readers' Advisory: exploring the implications of user-generated content for readers' advisory in Canadian public libraries, *Cataloging & Classification Quarterly*, **52** (4), 431–53.

Porter, J. (2011) Folksonomies in the Library: their impact on user experience, and their implications for the work of librarians, *Australian Library Journal*, **60** (3), 248–55.

RDA Steering Committee (n.d.) *RDA Basics*, http://rda-jsc.org/content/rda_faq#1.

Schultz-Jones, B., Snow, K., Miksa, S. and Hasenyager, R. (2012) Historical and Current Implications of Cataloging Quality for Next-Generation Catalogs, *Library Trends*, **61** (1), 49–82.

Smiraglia, R. P. (2009) Bibliocentrism, Cultural Warrant, and the Ethics of Resouce Description: a case study, *Cataloging & Classification Quarterly*, **47** (7), 671–86.

Spiteri, L. F. (2006) The Use of Folksonomies in Public Library Catalogues, *The Serials Librarian*, **51** (2), 75–89.

Spiteri, L. F. (2009) The Impact of Social Cataloguing Sites on the Construction of Bibliographic Records in the Public Library

Catalogue, *Cataloguing & Classification Quarterly*, **47** (1), 52–73.

Spiteri, L. F. (2012) Social Discovery Tools: extending the principle of user convenience, *Journal of Documentation*, **68** (2), 206–17.

Steele, T. (2009) The New Cooperative Cataloging, *Library Hi Tech*, **27** (1), 68–77.

Tarulli, L. and Spiteri, L. F. (2012) Library Catalogues of the Future: a social space and collaborative tool?, *Library Trends*, **61** (1), 107–31.

Thomas, M., Caudle, D. M. and Schmitz, C. M. (2009) To Tag or Not to Tag?, *Library Hi Tech*, **27** (3), 411–34.

Vander Wal, T. (2007) *Folksonomy*, 2 February, www.vanderwal.net/folksonomy.html.

West, W. (2013) Tag You're It: enhancing access to graphic novels, *Portal: Libraries & the Academy*, **13**, 301–24.

Notes

1 www.native-languages.org/iroquois_words.htm.
2 See https://twitter.com/hashtag/vegan?lang=en, www.instagram.com/explore/tags/vegan, www.facebook.com/hashtag/vegan and www.tumblr.com/tagged/vegan.

Index